Alfred Wallis
CORNISH PRIMITIVE

Alfred Wallis

CORNISH PRIMITIVE

Edwin Mullins

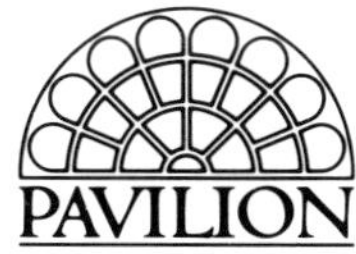

PAVILION

To all my St. Ives friends, past and present

First published in 1994 by
PAVILION BOOKS LIMITED
26 Upper Ground, London SE1 9PD

Designed by Nigel Partridge

A Conrad Goulden Book

A CIP catalogue record for this book is available from the British Library.

ISBN 1 85793 2749

Printed and bound in Spain by Cayfosa

2 4 6 8 10 9 7 5 3 1

This book may be ordered by post direct from the publisher. Please contact the
Marketing Department. But try your bookshop first.

Contents

AUTHOR'S NOTE   6

———

ALFRED WALLIS: PAINTER OF 'WHAT USED TO BE'   7

———

COLOUR PLATES   25

———

ACKNOWLEDGEMENTS   64

AUTHOR'S NOTE

In 1967 I wrote a book about Alfred Wallis which was a labour of love but which, through a quirk of the publishing trade, became unavailable almost the moment it saw the light of day. Several of the illustrations in this new book were originally obtained for that earlier publication. Since that time a number of paintings, as well as other material relating to Wallis, will have inevitably changed hands with no record of their present whereabouts. The Publishers and I have made every effort to trace the current owners of the works illustrated in this book. However, in a few cases we have been unable to do so and these are acknowledged by being marked 'Ex-collection' or simply 'Private collection'. We will happily undertake to correct any mis-attributions in future editions if the current owners would make themselves known to us.

The majority of Alfred Wallis' paintings remain in private hands, as are many of those reproduced in this book. The largest public collection may be seen at Kettle's Yard, University of Cambridge. Others are on display at the Tate Gallery, St. Ives and at the Pier Gallery, Stromness, Orkney.

PAINTER OF 'WHAT USED TO BE'

Alfred Wallis was born in Devonport near Plymouth in 1855. It was 'the day of the fall of Serveserpool Rushan War', he wrote with some pride since his father was away fighting in the Crimea at the time. His mother came from the Scilly Isles and died when Alfred was very young. The family was always poor, and he almost certainly never went to school.

Wallis claimed that at the age of nine he went to sea, first as a cabin-boy and then as a sailor on light Atlantic schooners and windjammers, sometimes crossing to North America on the early metal steamers and on the Newfound-

The St. Ives fishing fleet in the early 1900s, at the time when Wallis kept his Marine Stores on the harbour

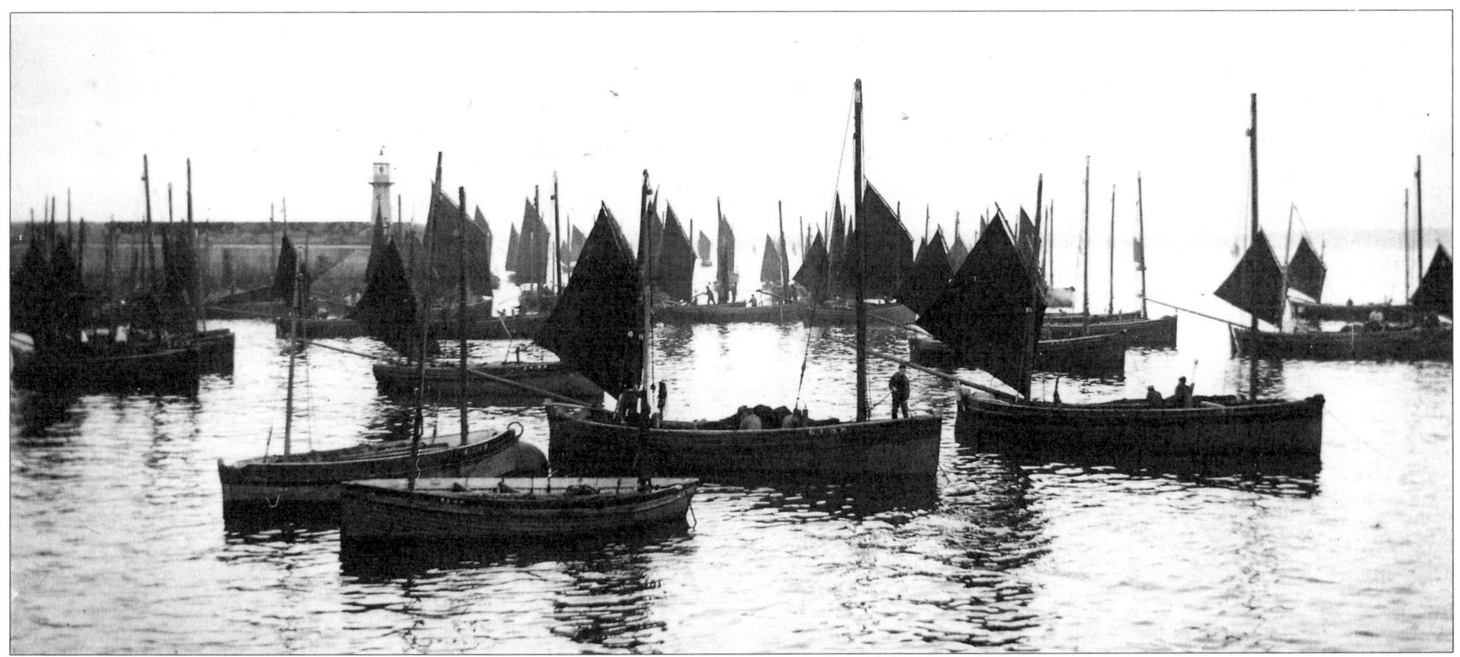

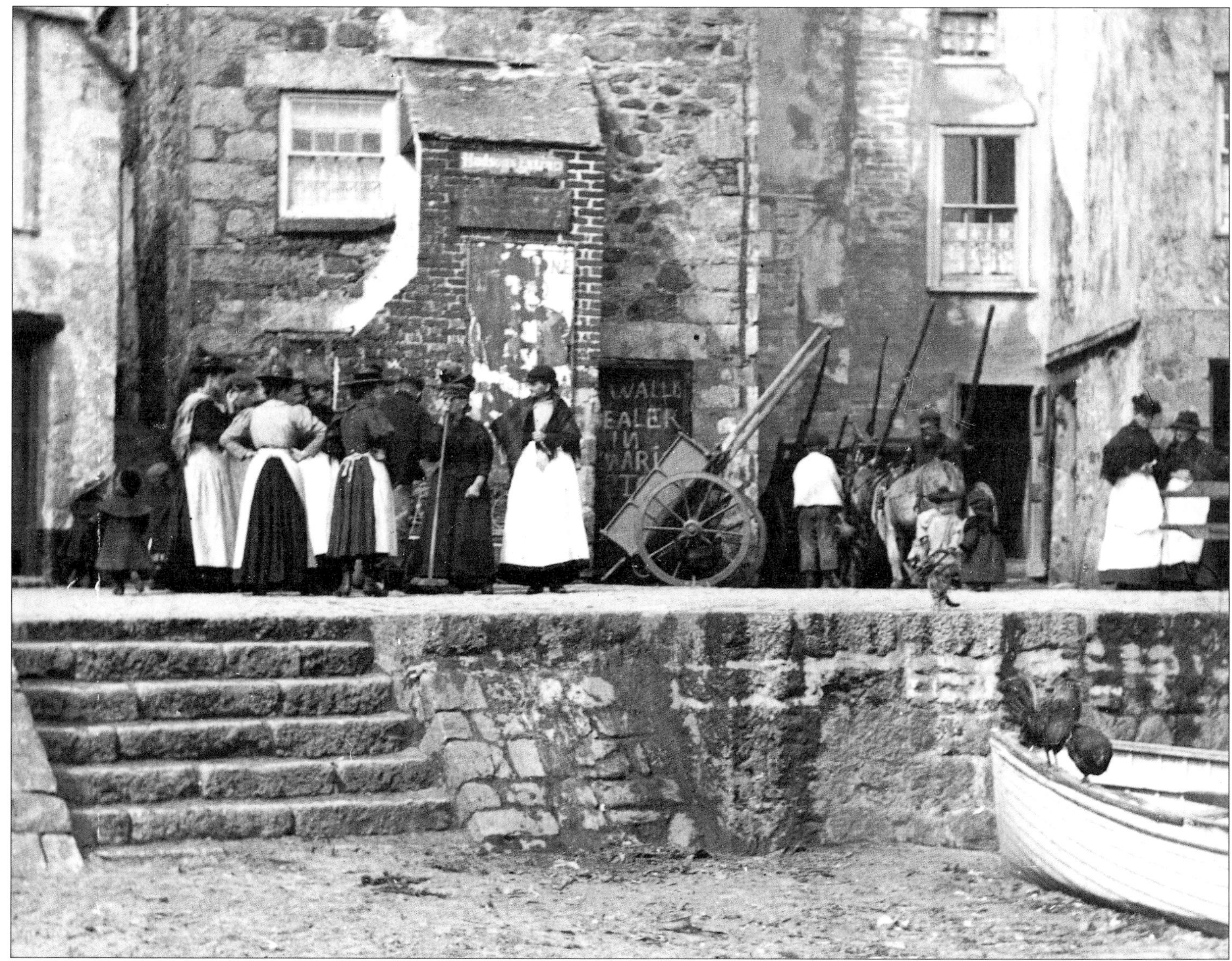

land boats known as Cod Bankers. In about 1880 he abandoned deep-sea fishing to become an inshore fisherman with the Newlyn and Mousehole fleets in search of pilchards, mackerel and herring according to the season. By this time he had moved to Penzance where in 1875 he had married Susan Agland. Wallis was then aged twenty, whereas Susan was a forty-one-year-old widow who had already borne seventeen children, of whom only five had survived. She proceeded to bear Wallis two more children, who also died.

By the late 1880s he seems to have abandoned fishing altogether. His brother Charles now ran a marine rag-and-bone business in Penzance, and in 1890 Wallis was persuaded to set up a similar business across the peninsula in St. Ives. As a result he and Susan moved there, first to No. 4 Bethesda Hill and then, as business flourished, on the harbour-front itself. Photographs survive of the little store down on the quayside, with its wooden door painted in clumsy white letters A WALLIS DEALER IN MARINE STORES, with the first 'N' written upside-down.

His rag-and-bone stores continued for more than twenty years. But with the arrival of steam-trawlers, the departure of the pilchards and the consequent decline of the Cornish

Wallis' Marine Stores on the harbour front in St. Ives, pre-1910. The diminutive white-jacketed figure between the donkey and donkey-cart is very possibly Wallis himself

fishing industry, business gradually fell away until Wallis abandoned it in 1912, moving with Susan into a tiny fisherman's cottage at No. 3 Back Road West, which he bought out of his savings. Here he scraped a living by making ice-cream and doing various odd jobs such as moving furniture and building government huts during the First World War.

Increasingly Wallis withdrew into himself, keeping company only with Susan, the newspapers and a large black family Bible which he would read aloud on Sundays. Then in 1922 Susan died, and Wallis was alone. Three years afterwards – by now aged seventy and receiving an Old Age Pension – he began to paint, 'for company' as he put it. Seventeen years later, in 1942, Wallis died in a workhouse near Penzance. He was eighty-seven.

I n his lifetime barely a dozen people appreciated his paintings: mostly he was regarded in St. Ives as somewhat odd, which in his old age he undoubtedly was. Not being a local man but a 'foreigner' from Devonshire, Wallis had never quite fitted into the community and, suspicious by nature, he had few friends. Yet he was widely remembered as a character, and was the subject of many a bizarre tale.

During the 1950s and 60s a St. Ives general practitioner, Dr. Roger Slack, became intrigued by the many accounts of

Wallis which his patients volunteered at his surgery, and decided to record on tape their recollections of the man.

They are precious memories. Here are some of them.

————

'He was a marvellous little chap. Little short chap. Always had a watery eye, like he had weak eyes, you know . . . I can see him now, he used to have one of these here red spotty handkerchiefs wiping his eyes; they used to run terrible, you know. I've seen his eyes bloodshot. He was a very sprightly man. He was small, but he was very quick.'

(*Jacob Ward – step-grandson*)

————

'He used to take long walks. Nothing for him to walk to Penzance and back. Very long walks. He was a very active little fellow, you know. Oh, he was very springy on his legs – springy!'

(*Sarah Langford – neighbour in Back Road West*)

————

'He had a little harmonium and it was no bigger than this. And he would sit down and try to sing, and Grandma would say to him "For goodness sake, Alfred, put it down. You can go up to the [Salvation] Army to sing. Don't sing here".'

(*Nancy Ward – second wife of Wallis' stepson*)

'Dapper little man, you know. Long jersey on, and he thought all the girls in St. Ives were after him. Oh yes, he was a dapper little man. He had a gold watch, handsome gold watch. He used to take it to the jewellers every week and have it wound.'

(*Thomas Cothey – neighbour in Back Road West*)

————

'After she died, Mr. Wallis never slept upstairs no more. Never went upstairs. He said the devil was upstairs, and he never went up there. He made up a bed in behind the table, because he was a very small man, you know – Oh, a very small man.'

(*Sarah Langford*)

————

'Just a poor boy before the mast, what they call. He did go to sea. And he's been in my mother's house and telling my grandfather all about his experiences. He was a little cabin-boy in one of the big boats – I suppose in those days it was the three-mast ships. And he told 'im he wasn't more than nine or ten when he was in the Bay of Biscay. . . . He been out there where the sharks are, you know. . . . My grandfather, he was very old, he was over seventy, and one day he met in with Granda Wallis at the bottom, and they got talking. And he came in and said to my mother, "Ellen, you don't seem to have a very good opinion of that little man, but he's a jolly nice little chap. And I've asked him to come in and spend an hour or two in the evenings and have a bit of a talk".'

(Nancy Ward)

———

'We had lots of little connections with him as boys. He was a Marine Dealer, but I don't think he was a St. Ives man. He had his Marine Stores down on the wharf. The store was in a kind of cellar. He lived over. Course he used to buy any kinds of metal, iron or rags and bones. As boys we wasn't very well off for Saturdays' spending money, and we used to go on the beaches and collect small quantities of rags and bones – there were four of us. But they had to be clean, and he wouldn't have old bones with meat on them. Then we used to take them up there and he would take a look at them and probably might say "tuppence". We would probably think them worth a ha'penny more and try and drive a bargain. But if Mr Wallis said "tuppence", it was tuppence. . . . He was a quiet man, an industrious man: he could do lots of things apart from that.'

(Thomas Lander – former St. Ives fisherman, later a coal-miner)

———

'We were all kids there together. He never used to make much of us, more huffy like; didn't seem to have much patience with children. The old lady was nice, a dear old soul. He was different altogether: he was rough. He used to chase us, especially boys who brought iron and bones in buckets: he used to give them a ha'penny or a penny. Of course when his back was turned they would take them again and resell them; then he would chase them.'

(Carrie Lander – wife of Thomas Lander, as a child lived close to Wallis' Marine Stores)

———

'He had a good business down on the wharf, see. I can see my granny down there now, sorting out the stuff, the cottons from the woollens. I can remember the little pony he had – Albert he was called.'

(Jessie Farrell – step-granddaughter)

———

'Once upon a time he made ice-cream. Somebody brought this recipe for this ice-cream, I've got to think, I think somebody trading to Italy on a ship brought the recipe home and he used to make it. He had an ice-cream barrow; push it sometimes to Penzance to sell ice-cream, I suppose on certain days – market days. Quite a long way to push a barrow, I should think.'

(George Farrell – son of Jessie Farrell)

'I said to him one day, "Well, 'ere, 'ow did you learn to be an artist instead of a rag-and-bone man, then?" He said, "I didn't have more sense than that." And I said, "Well, 'ow do you come to do this, then?" He said, "I had a bit of cardboard here one day." And the paints he had were children's little, small, little – you know – tuppenny, threepenny things of painting. And he said he started to draw little small pictures. Several people had them from him, and he gave them to the children. . . . You'd hear somebody say, "Everything in Mr Wallis' is nothing but boats. He's painting up everything." He did too. I used to wonder at the artists going in there so much, you know; they would go in and they would carry in wood, you know for him to paint on – pictures. We used to say, "Well, what do they see in that picture?" Of course we've known since that he was the cleverest artist around. He would have a tin of paint and a paintbrush, and he'd go for it.'

(*Nancy Ward*)

————

'He used to be forever painting. He used to have, Oh, he used to paint on the table and on the wall, paint on anything that you gave him. Funny thing everybody used to think that he was eccentric, you know, but nobody took much interest in his paintings. . . . He used to have a passion for painting mackerel boats, you know, mackerel luggers, double-end mackerel luggers, and they used to be used to make a frieze of them all the way along the wainscotting. . . . He used to paint on everything; he used to paint on the cups as well – nothing was safe from where paint could go like. . . . I think he used to use any kind of paint he could get hold of. I don't think he ever used the correct articles. If he had grey paint he used grey paint. If he had blue he used blue. . . . Never flowers, but nearly always a ship, you know, as if to say he could never get away from it, you know – something that always followed him, you know.'

(*George Farrell*)

————

'Being deaf, you had to do all the talking, but he was never a saucy man nor nothing like that. And he wouldn't have any paint only the yacht paint; called it "yacht paint for the boats, see." . . . He'd only buy little cheap camel hair brushes, you know: you can't press on them or anything, can you? . . . He said, "I don't use the paint artists use; mine's the *real* paint. Don't want the muck they've got".'

(*Joe Burrell – painter-decorator and neighbour*)

————

'He used to explain his work to anyone who really wanted to know, but once he found out that you were trying to take the mickey out of him, or a ride, you would never have anything

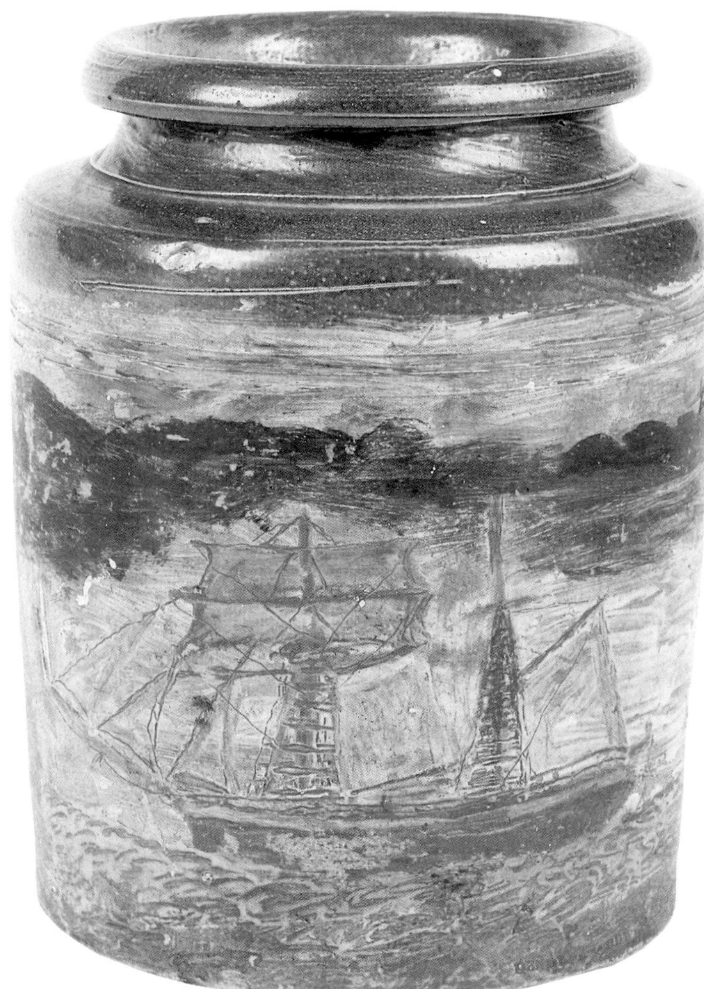

Painted marmalade jar

more to do with Alfred. While you played the game he was all right.'
(Thomas Lander)

———

'When my granny died my mother used to make dinner for him. . . . And every time I went in he used to say, "'ere you are, my child, carry this 'ome." Well, it was like a stone jar, like we used to get the marmalade in those days, was stone jars. But they were all boats and all, painted around this. Well, I used to carry them home. Mother used to say to me, "Well, don't for heaven's sake Emily bring any more of them in because – throw them in the dustbin." . . . The stone jars, I've had scores of them, see. . . . Never gave us any money or anything like that. Never pass any money. But you could have a jar or a piece of cardboard with a boat or at sea.'
(Emily Woolcock – granddaughter of Susan Wallis)

———

'And Willie used to carry his dinner every day, and when we used to leave the plates there, and little basins with his dinner, he used to draw on them and paint. My mother didn't know they were any good. She used to wash them off – took a lot to wash them off. . . . Ben Nicholson brought a canvas there for him to paint on. He used to paint with the views of a child because – as he saw – that's how modern art came in.'
(Jessie Farrell)

'*I* went in there and he was in one of his moods, and he was in there painting. You couldn't disturb him when he was painting, and I put the dinner on the table and he told me to get out plate and all and I had to carry it back to Aunt Jessie. . . . But he was a wonderful old chap in his time: I can't see nothing missing from Grandfather Wallis.'

(*Jacob Ward*)

———

'*He* used to be queer at times. And you'd knock on the door and it would open a crack as if the burglars were expected at any minute. Then we used to come in. . . . Sometimes he would let you watch him a bit, and he used to have luggers painted all around the table and on the wall, you know. And oh, I always remember he kept the teapot in the oven and it used to be pretty strong by the time he got it out. But he was certainly queer. . . . I don't know why he developed a passion for painting like he did. . . . Ever since I can remember he painted on everything, and you could have had the paintings for nothing. He painted on cardboard, anything he could get hold of.'

(*George Farrell*)

———

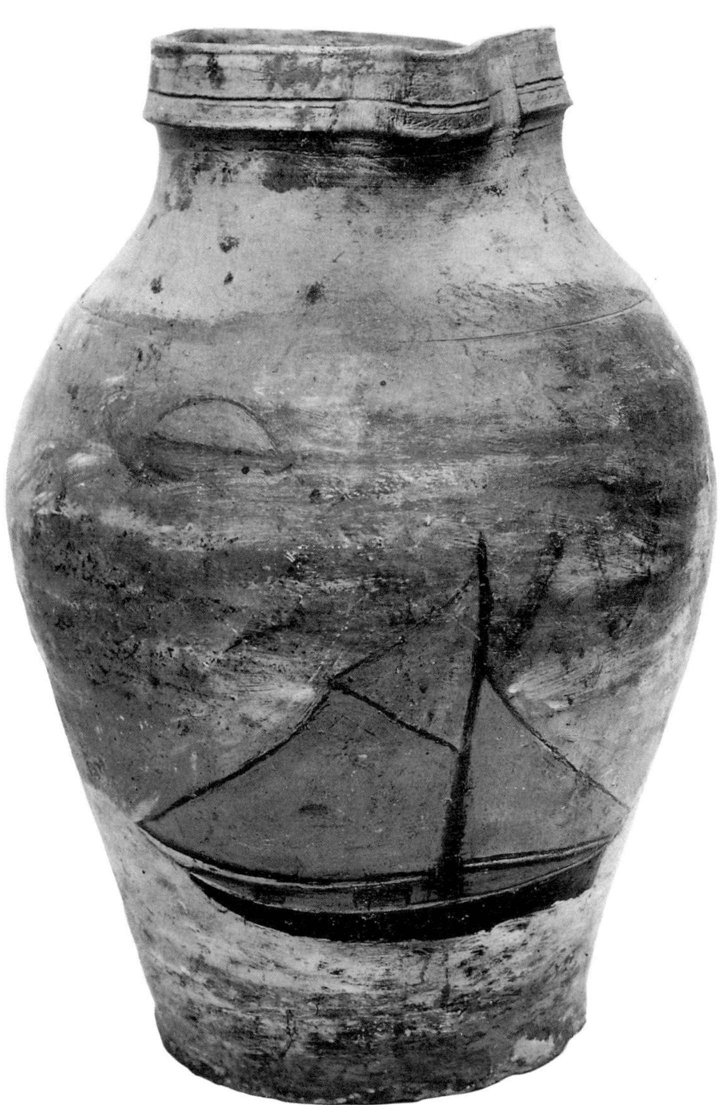

Painted earthenware pitcher. Wallis regularly painted on anything he could lay his hands on

'*He* did go funny, he did. I used to say, "Granda, why don't you come up and live with we? You've got the little room; that'll be your room, and don't worry you'll have plenty of company up with we." "No! I aren't going to give up my own house to live with nobody." Then he sold his house for about forty pound, but for the length of time while he lived he stayed there. . . . Oh, went awful dirty, though. . . . I felt it awful to see that old man put away, I did. I felt it something awful. And my husband used to say, "You're feeling more for 'ee than what my sisters are." "Well," I said, "they haven't got no more sense than that. No," I said, "I can't see him going to the poorhouse." But he did. He went in there.'

(*Nancy Ward*)

———•———

The words 'primitive' and 'naive' are convenient labels, but when applied to Alfred Wallis they can be misleading without some qualification. A distinction needs to be made between naiveté of technique and naiveté of vision. Most painters who are dubbed 'primitive' or 'naive' present a vision of a brightly-coloured world that is essentially childlike and innocent, a Garden of Eden before the Fall, and yet technically their work is often meticulous and in its own way highly sophisticated.

By contrast Wallis' paintings are anything but childlike and innocent: what he offers is a passionate and adult vision of a way of life which he once experienced, and is now remembering. His technique on the other hand is untrained and intuitive: Wallis improvises much as a gifted child will improvise, grasping whatever materials happen to be at hand and making imaginative uses of them such as few sophisticated adults would even think of. Instead of a sophisticated technique being placed in the service of a childlike vision, with Wallis it is the other way round: the free imagination of a child serves to illuminate the profoundly-felt experience of an adult world.

It is this unusual combination of talents which gives Wallis his distinctive quality as an artist, linking him not only to other untutored artists such as 'le Douanier' Rousseau, but just as strongly to modern masters like Klee, Chagall, Miro, Dubuffet and in certain phases of their careers, Picasso and Matisse, as well as to the two English artists who first discovered him – Christopher Wood and Ben Nicholson. With the extraordinary self-confidence of his own instincts, Wallis hit on one of the principal tenets of modern art, namely that painting is a visual language designed to record not so much how the world looks as how it *feels*: the primacy of imagination and personal experience over acquired technique.

Wallis was a man locked up darkly within himself. For the last seventeen years of his life painting became virtually his sole occupation, as well as the only outlet for his deeper emotions. By nature he was proud, irascible, austere and somewhat misanthropic. In his old age painting was his only constant friend and to this activity he was entirely – and passionately – dedicated. It was a dedication to creating a pictorial record of the world as he once knew it and which no one would ever see again.

Primarily this was a world which centred on man's experience of the sea, recalled from an era when the Cornish fishing industry was at its zenith. By the time Wallis began to paint, in the 1920s, that industry had all but died. He could remember the days when St. Ives harbour had been crammed with mackerel boats; when the three-masters would set out from Penzance for the cod-banks off Newfoundland, and the tall schooners load their cargoes of Cornish pilchards for Italy. And he could remember how every able-bodied man in St. Ives would rush to lend a hand whenever a school of pilchards came near to shore.

Wallis' paintings are the product of a kind of obsession; an obsession to recall what he believed to have been real and true about the world of his younger days. He didn't try to glamorize it or to decorate it with his own fanciful inventions: what his brush recorded was simply 'what used to Bee out of my own memery'. Ben Nicholson, who knew him well, has emphasized that Wallis never considered his paintings as paintings so much as *actual events*. Each picture was a re-living of some valuable experience and he knew precisely the occasion of that experience and its significance. If he felt communicative – which was rare but not unknown – he would sometimes place his paintings outside his cottage and 'explain to you what they were: details of sails, what every part was used for, and the ropes', as one St. Ives inhabitant remembered. Nicholson has written of one visit he made to Wallis' cottage when he enquired the meaning of a large, fierce-looking fish which was as big as a fishing-boat but apparently floundering on the edge of the sea. 'He stopped talking,' Nicholson recalled, 'his face lit up with the most charming expression and he shrugged his shoulders. "That," he said, "that's a land-shark", and he went on smiling for a long time after that.'

Wallis always made a point of saying he never went out of the house to paint. This was important to him. It was part of the distinction he carefully drew between himself and the trained painters of St. Ives who had studios a short distance from his own cottage. They painted what they *saw*, whereas he painted 'out of my own memery'. Neither did he use the conventional materials of a painter – canvas and artists' oils. This was partly because he couldn't afford them; but more particularly it was a matter of personal choice. Wallis was careful only to use the things he understood, and he was

The fishing fleet setting out from St. Ives, early 1900s, when the local fishing industry was still at its height

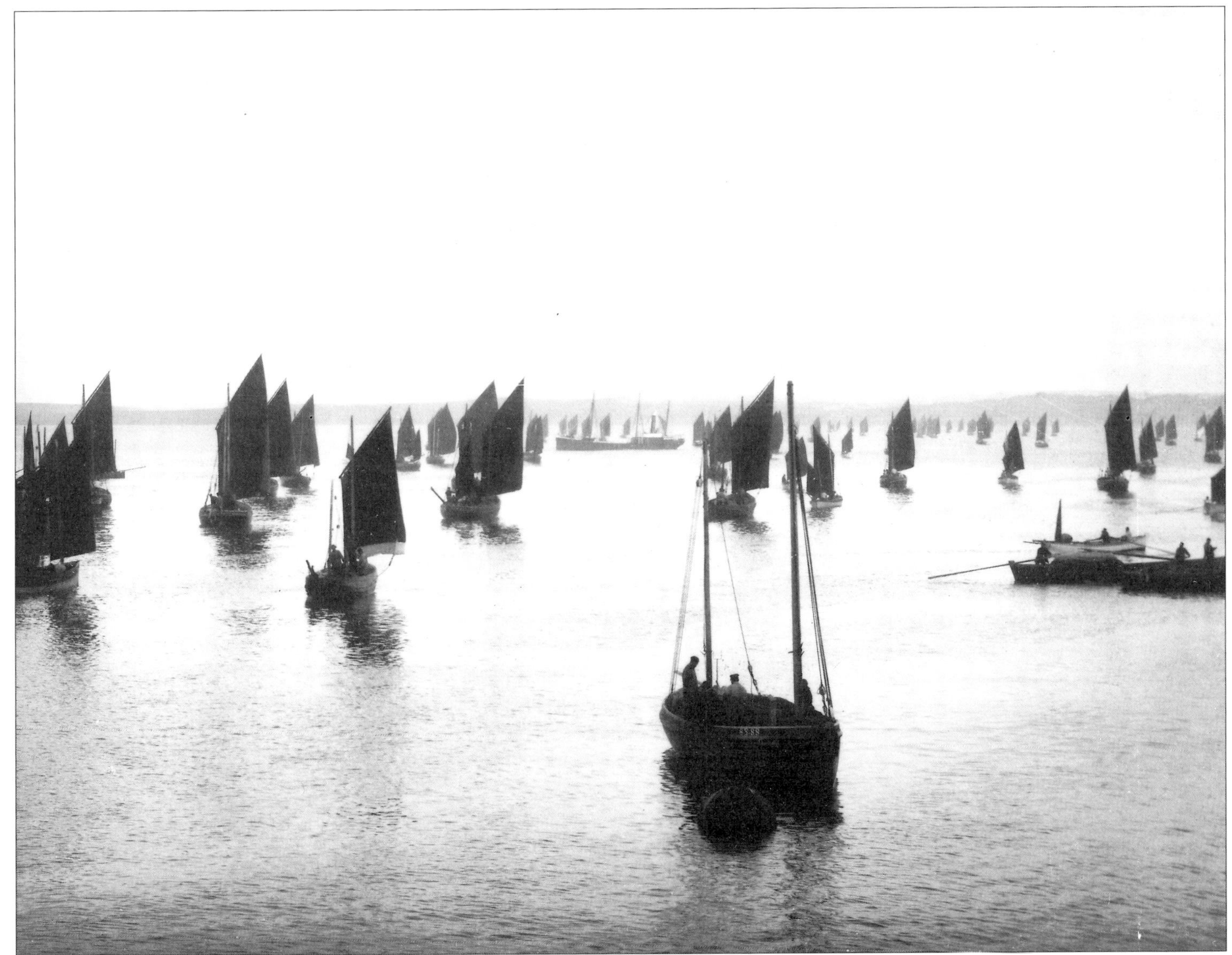

deeply suspicious of anything else. As one of his neighbours remembers him saying, 'I don't use the paints artists use; mine's the *real* paint. Don't want the muck they've got.'

Equally unlike the methods of the professional artists around him was the way he worked. His customary practice was to work on a flat table in his little downstairs room in Back Road West whose door led directly on to the street. This is how Christopher Wood and Ben Nicholson found him in 1928 when they passed the old man's door by chance and saw him working at his table looking 'just like Cézanne', as Wood described him.

One feature of the way he worked is that images tend to be arranged according to their significance rather than for the sake of topographical accuracy. Looking at a Wallis painting it is often easy to pick out what was the central image in the artist's mind and to see how other images are bent round it, frequently reduced in size and pushed away round the edges of the picture. This central image is most often a boat, though it may also be a tree, a particular house, a bridge, a harbour or a lighthouse. No painting is just a scene, or a view; it is about something particular, something upon which a story may hang. And a picture was his way of telling that story.

As a result, his paintings are never purely descriptive; they are designed to tell us what matters. When he paints the sea he is concerned to convey what it feels like to *be* at sea – to be out in a small boat tossed about by the waves, or by contrast to be back within the enclosing arms of a harbour. Wallis' use of paint is never more vigorous or more imaginative than when conveying the moods and textures of water. What he creates is a seaman's vision of the ocean. He can stir

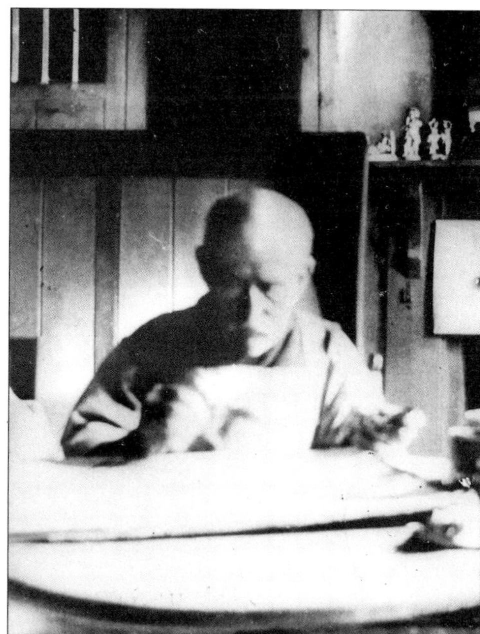

Alfred Wallis painting in his cottage at Back Road West, St. Ives during the 1930s

up his paint into a boiling, frothy substance to suggest a storm. Or the paint can be as thick as cement, as brown and sluggish as beer, or sharp as scythes flailing up over a boat's prow. At other times it is transparent in order to reveal gigantic fish that swim beneath or the wreck of a sunken ship on the rocks. Just occasionally, as if to show that a seaman's life is not all storms, he will paint a tranquil blue surface over which a boat glides serenely and white gulls fly.

Because Wallis was a storyteller it was sometimes important to him to explain his paintings by awarding them elaborate titles. There is an all-green landscape with houses, birds and various animals who include a striped beast and on the back of the picture the inscription reads, 'Their was a donkey sold by Aucton fetched 2000 pounds ad stripes like one duren The war i Saw very scarce To see one with stripes'.

Another painting, in the Kettle's Yard collection, bears a similarly factual title, 'Consols Mine Raswall Hill and the Road Zennor and Farms The White you see is Granite', while on the front of the picture, written round the edge, run the words 'This is a quary of granet'. The whole scene is viewed from the air as if it were a pictorial map. The comparison is apt: with old pictorial maps it was common for a cartographer to distort the shape of a country or a stretch of coastline in the interests of fitting it into the sheet of parchment, as well as leaving out what seemed unimportant.

This is precisely how Wallis appears to have regarded a good many of his own paintings. Like maps, they have no fixed viewpoint: one makes a journey within them and around them, just as Wallis himself must have done when painting them. He worked from above, on a flat table-top and often from all sides, bending his subject into whatever shape of board he was using and concentrating only on the salient features that concerned him.

The more important these features were, the larger they tend to be. Scale had as little meaning to Wallis as perspective. Just as in early Christian paintings the figures of Christ and the Virgin Mary frequently dwarf all surrounding figures, Wallis' own priorities are reflected in similar distortions. The fish and dolphins which sport around his ships are sometimes almost as large as the ships themselves. Cliffs soar up and out of paintings as if to evoke the experience of cliffs seen looking up from a small boat. His boats heel all over the place. Some are on their sides. Others climb up at a steep angle. Sometimes there is more than one horizontal plane in a single picture and ships appear to be sailing on a series of shelves one above the other. In many of his paintings the sea is far higher at one end of a boat than it is at the other.

Accompanying these distortions of scale and perspective is a remarkable instinct for pictorial design. Wallis was deeply sensitive to the shapes of things — not only of the images he was painting but the shapes of the cardboard fragments on which he generally worked. Wallis never bought

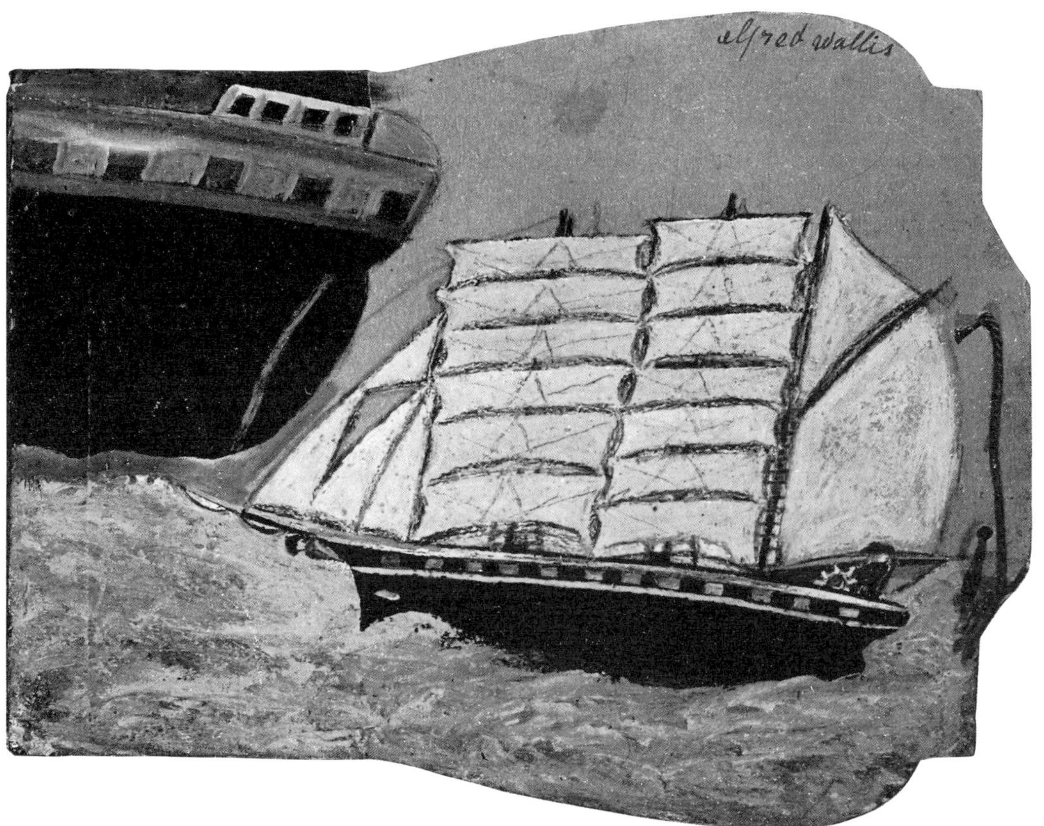

Three-master, painted on the back of a calendar. Wallis always chose to make use of irregularly shaped board rather than trim it into a neat rectangle

canvases: he couldn't possibly have afforded to. He used whatever came his way – scraps of board which the grocer saved for him, paper of different colours, bits of packing-cases, old calendars, a blotter, shoe boxes, Quaker Oats boxes (he was particularly fond of these). All of them tended to be irregular in shape and ragged-edged; but instead of trimming them into neat rectangles as one might have expected, Wallis chose to incorporate these irregularities into the design of each picture, arranging his subject-matter so that it fitted into the shape of the board and in turn became enhanced by it.

The result is that Wallis' pictures give off a powerful sense of rhythm, with images creating strong formal patterns which are themselves echoed by the shapes they are painted on. The rounded corners of a piece of board match the billowing sails of fishing-boats. An expanse of rough sea parts in the very centre of a picture to reveal a sailing-ship. The effect is startling, evoking a mood of isolation and loneliness as if the ship were trapped within the open mouth of the ocean.

When the grocer gave him board to paint on, Wallis made use not only of its irregular edges but of its natural texture and colour. In a great many of his pictures there are areas he left deliberately blank, especially round the sails of his boats or in patches of sky, sometimes just dabbling in a few stray clouds here and there. 'i thought it not nessery to paint it all round so i never Don it', Wallis wrote in a letter to H. S. Ede, who formed what is today the Kettle's Yard collection in Cambridge, and who at that time (1929) was an Assistant at the Tate Gallery in London. It sounds so natural a solution, to use the material he was working on as part of the finished colour-scheme, so making the board an integral part of the picture. It was to become common practice among *collage* artists and was to be extensively used by Ben Nicholson. But Wallis knew nothing of these things; he was entirely unaware of what other artists were doing outside St. Ives, and hit upon the idea purely by instinct.

It was instinct, too, that caused Wallis to restrict his colours to a narrow range – a variety of browns, a rich black,
a vivid green, occasionally a little pink and yellow and, most of all, to a wide mix of greys and whites for the sea. 'i do not put Collers what do not Belong', Wallis wrote with his usual self-assurance to Ede in 1935, 'i Think it spoils The pictures Their have Been a lot of paintins spoiled By putin Collers where They do not Blong.'

Wallis used ordinary ships' paint, never artists' oils. This limited his scope, but it suited him so. He would use what colours he chanced to have, which were always very few; as a result many of his best paintings are keyed to a single dominant colour, which was either the colour of the board he was working on, or one that he chose to apply himself.

Subsidiary colours he would key to the principal one, just as he would arrange certain images so that they became subsidiary to the central one. If he worked on a greenish paper he would allow the green to show through here and there like a light shining from beneath; then he would enhance the effect by adding further touches of green to the sea, the mast, or the sails. He would do the same with pink or brown paper. At other times, instead of allowing the board or paper he worked on to dictate the master-colour, he would first of all apply an overall layer of a chosen shade and then proceed to treat it in precisely the same way, overpainting it with a few colours while always ensuring that the master-colour remained dominant.

Certain colours are predictable with Wallis. Rocks are

invariably a dark, sticky-looking chocolate-brown. The turf on the cliffs above the rocks and the fields beyond are what Nicholson has described as 'a particularly pungent Cornish green'. Blossom is always as a child paints it: a dab of white with a coloured centre. The sea is most often a thick iron grey composed of numerous shades between black and white superimposed in glazes one upon another.

Wallis also drew a lot, especially in the last years of his life when he was in the workhouse at Madron, near Penzance, and didn't always have the paints he wanted. There are a number of sketchbooks which date from this period – the early 1940s – and they are filled with drawings of ships, porpoises and great sweeping gulls in flight. But his most effective use of the pencil was in his actual paintings. Here he would frequently draw in the rigging and the outline of sails on top of the wet paint, so that the point of the pencil (or sometimes the sharp end of a paint-brush) dug into the surface and gave the picture a tactile, three-dimensional quality.

If it seems remarkable that Wallis should have become a painter at all, it is equally remarkable that so much of his work should have survived. We know that much of it has *not*

Letter from Wallis to his chief patron, H. S. Ede, 6 April 1935. Explanatory letters of this kind would accompany parcels of paintings sent to Ede when he was an assistant at the Tate Gallery in London, over a period of many years

Ap 6 1935
Dear Sir i Receved
your letter With Thanks
and also The pantins Wich you
Did not want
what i do Mosley is what
use To Bee out of my own
memery what we May never
see again as Thing are altered
all To gether Ther is nothin
what Ever do not look like
what it was sence i Can kember
if i live Till The 8 of august
next i shall Be 78 years old
i was Born in Devenport
Born on The day of The fall
of Serveserpool Rushan
So i Cos from your war
friend alfred wallis

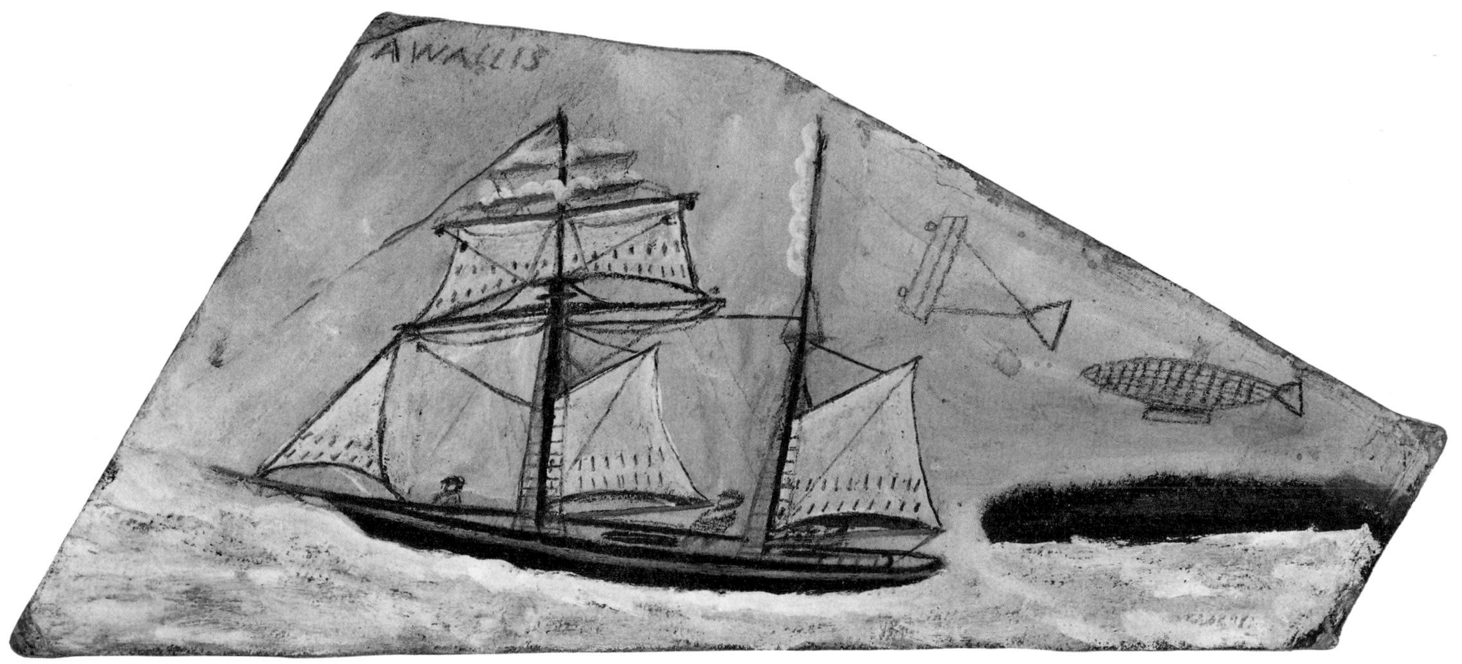

Sailing ship, aeroplane and airship

survived — the rueful stories of paintings burnt on rubbish-dumps and of painted marmalade-jars tipped into dustbins. He was appreciated by only a few. Where he was fortunate was that those few were people of discernment and influence: they were people whose opinions carried weight. The majority of them were themselves distinguished artists, who saw in what Wallis was doing by instinct a strong affinity with their own more conscious endeavours.

It was largely through the efforts of such artists, Ben Nicholson above all, that Wallis' small circle of admirers grew steadily during the last decade of his life. Nicholson's first wife, Winifred, had always been an enthusiastic supporter. His second wife, Barbara Hepworth, caught her husband's enthusiasm just as strongly. The art critic Herbert Read was another who came into contact with Wallis at this time and acquired some of his work. Others included the artist Peter Lanyon, the potter Bernard Leach, and the Russian sculptor Naum Gabo (who had moved to St. Ives at the outbreak of war).

Then there was H. S. Ede, another collector encouraged by Nicholson to take an interest in Wallis. Ede never actually met the painter, but corresponded with him regularly and would receive hefty packages of his paintings through the post while he was an Assistant at the Tate Gallery. After Ede left the country to live in Morocco in 1936, Wallis' most faithful supporters became the painter Adrian Stokes and his wife Margaret Mellis. It was Stokes who arranged for Wallis' funeral, and for his grave in Porthmeor Cemetery and who managed to dissuade the St. Ives Relieving Officer from ordering the hundreds of paintings left behind in Wallis' cottage to be burnt along with the fleas and the filth. Stokes has described how he just dumped the lot in his own garage – and ran.

The last phase of Wallis' life is rather tragic. He could not avoid the end he dreaded – to die in the workhouse. Yet in the enclosed world of Madron Institution he became something of a celebrity. Alethea Garstin has recounted a touching story of him there. She visited the place in 1941 and in one of the long rooms where the inmates lived 'there was this old prophet – they had let his hair grow long – and the others were looking at him with reverence. They were sweet to him, and one of them said to me in a serious tone of voice – "This gentleman is an artist!"'

Wallis died on 29 August 1942 and at his own request was given a Salvation Army funeral. This took place on 3 September. Ben Nicholson, Barbara Hepworth, Naum Gabo and his wife, Adrian Stokes and his wife and Bernard Leach, were among those who attended the ceremony. The local paper records that a floral tribute was sent by Mr. and Mrs. Naum Gabo with the following words, 'In homage to the artist on

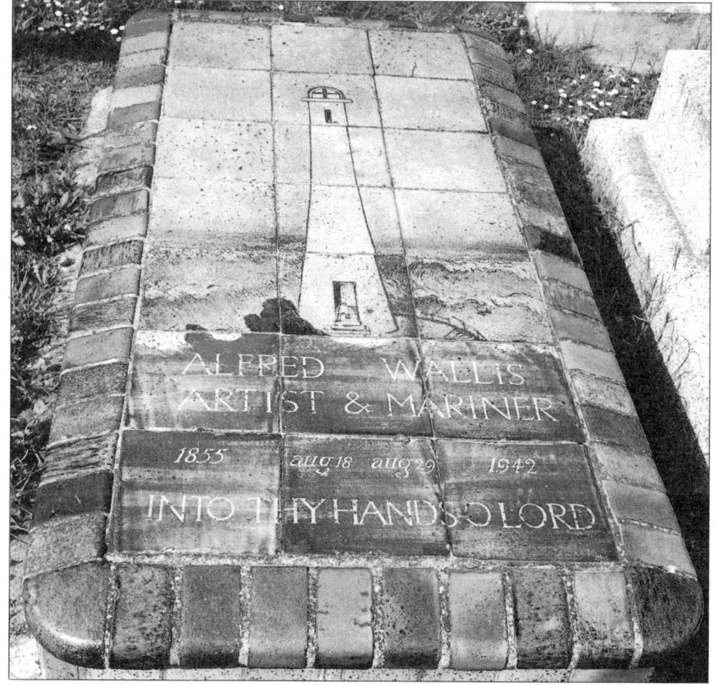

Alfred Wallis' grave in St. Ives, decorated with tiles by Bernard Leach

whom Nature has bestowed the rarest of gifts, not to know that he is one'.

The artists who visited him in his lifetime clubbed together to save him a pauper's burial. The grave in Porthmeor Cemetery is a raised slab covered with tiles made specially for the occasion by Bernard Leach. He decorated them in the form of a tall lighthouse buffeted by the waves. Leading up to it are steps which a little man with a stick is climbing; and on the grave are inscribed the words 'Alfred Wallis, Artist and Mariner'.

COLOUR PLATES

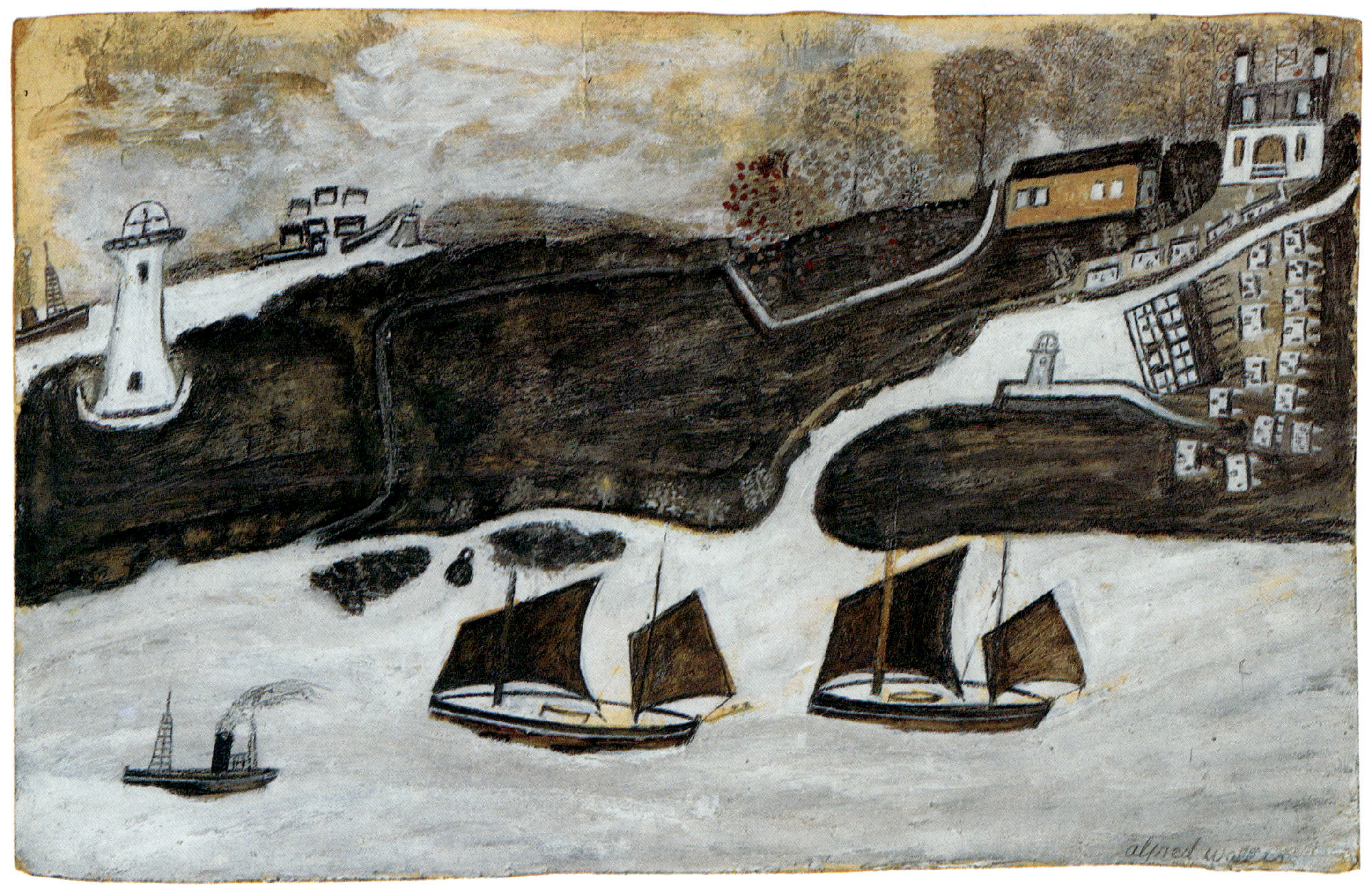

Fishing boats and lighthouse

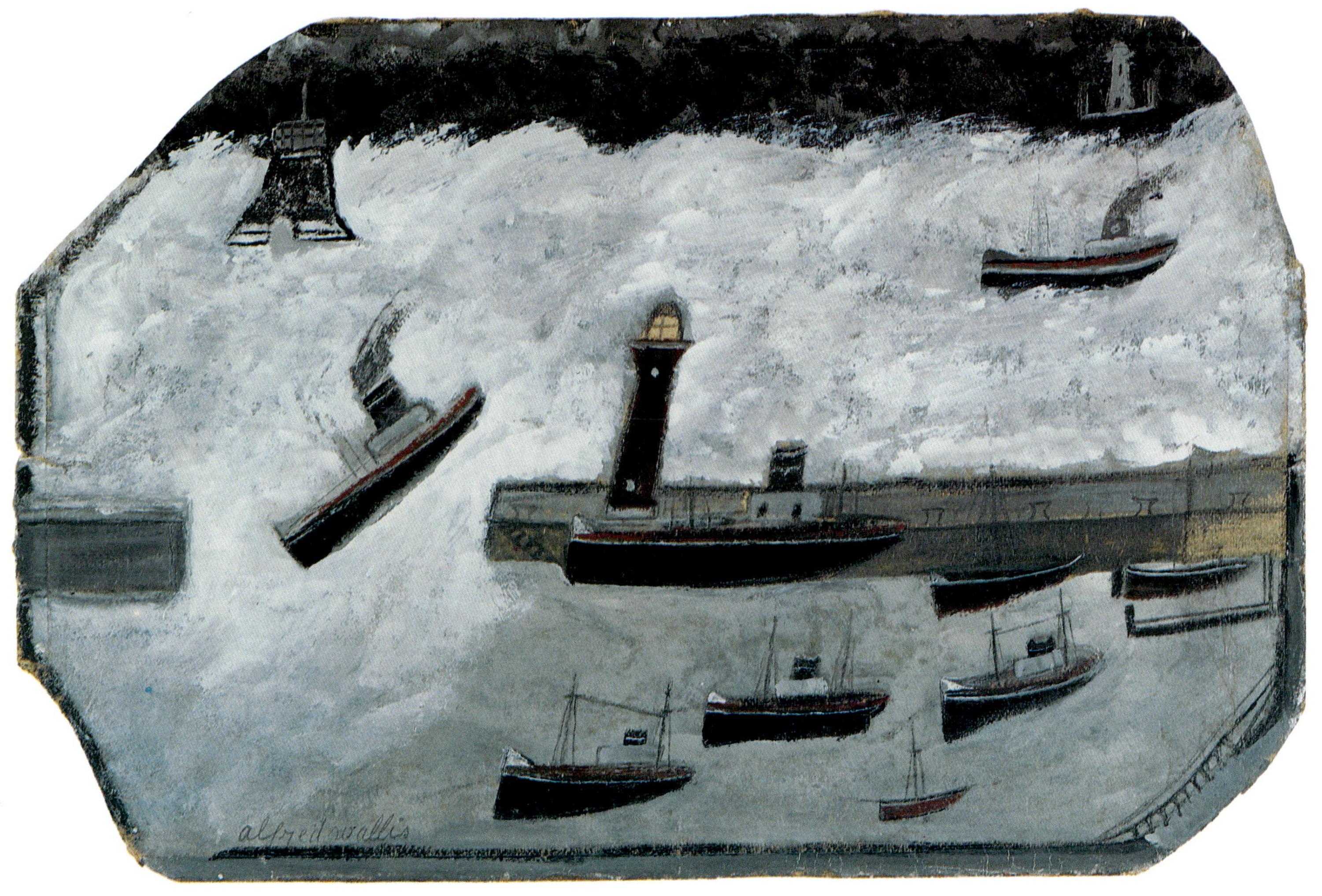

Penzance harbour. In the background is a diminutive version
of St. Michael's Mount

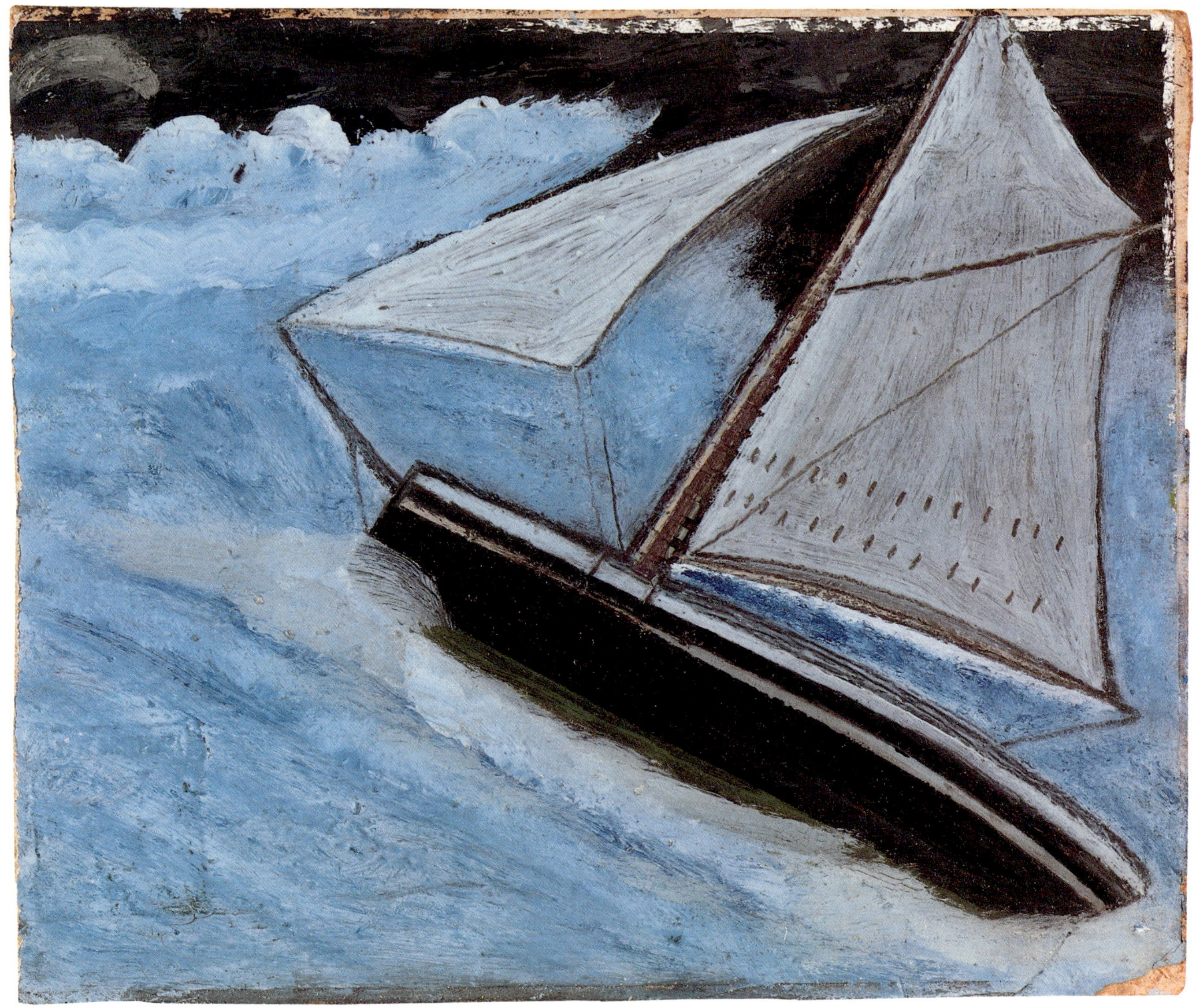

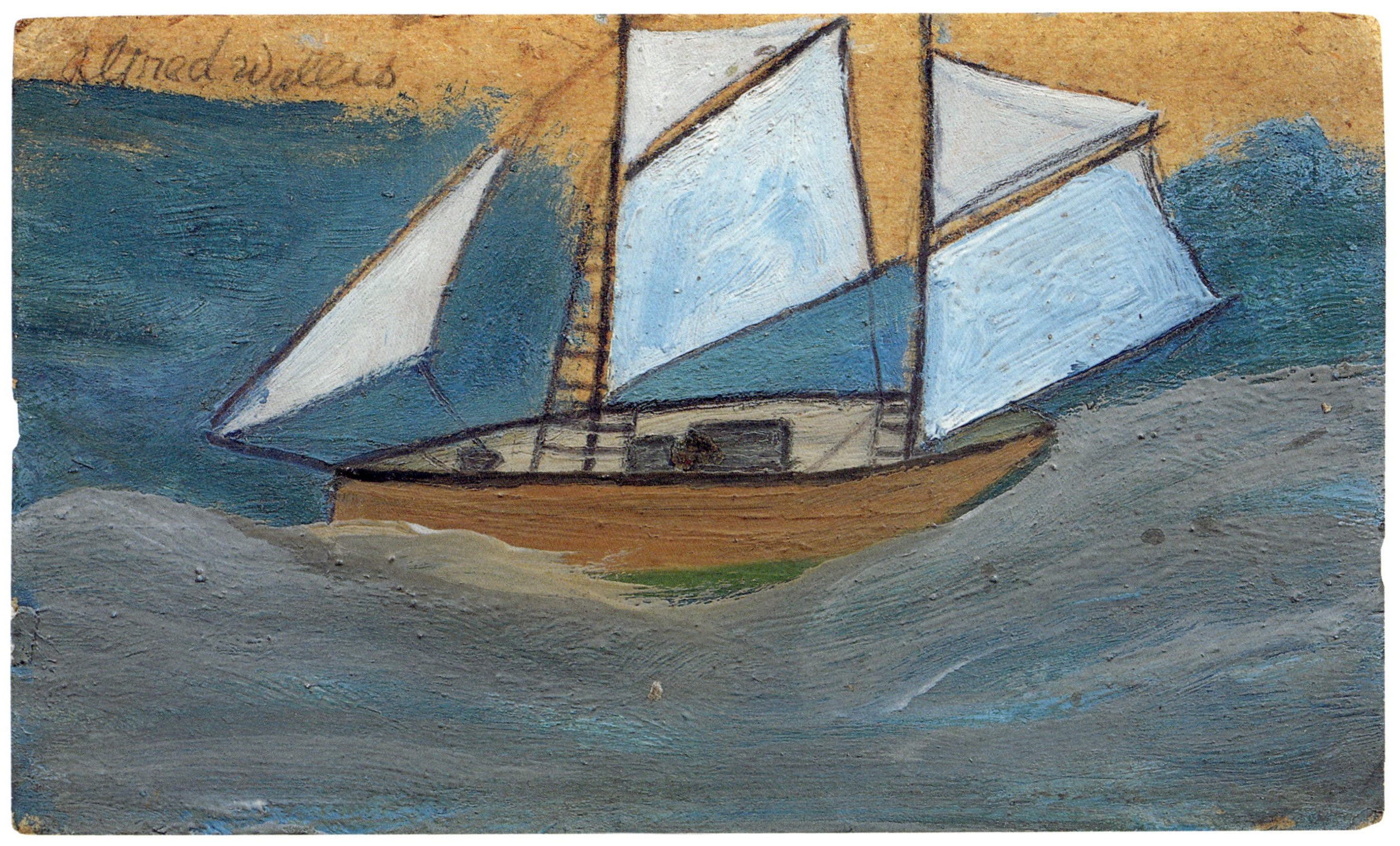

ABOVE Ships in a rough sea

LEFT Small boat in a rough sea

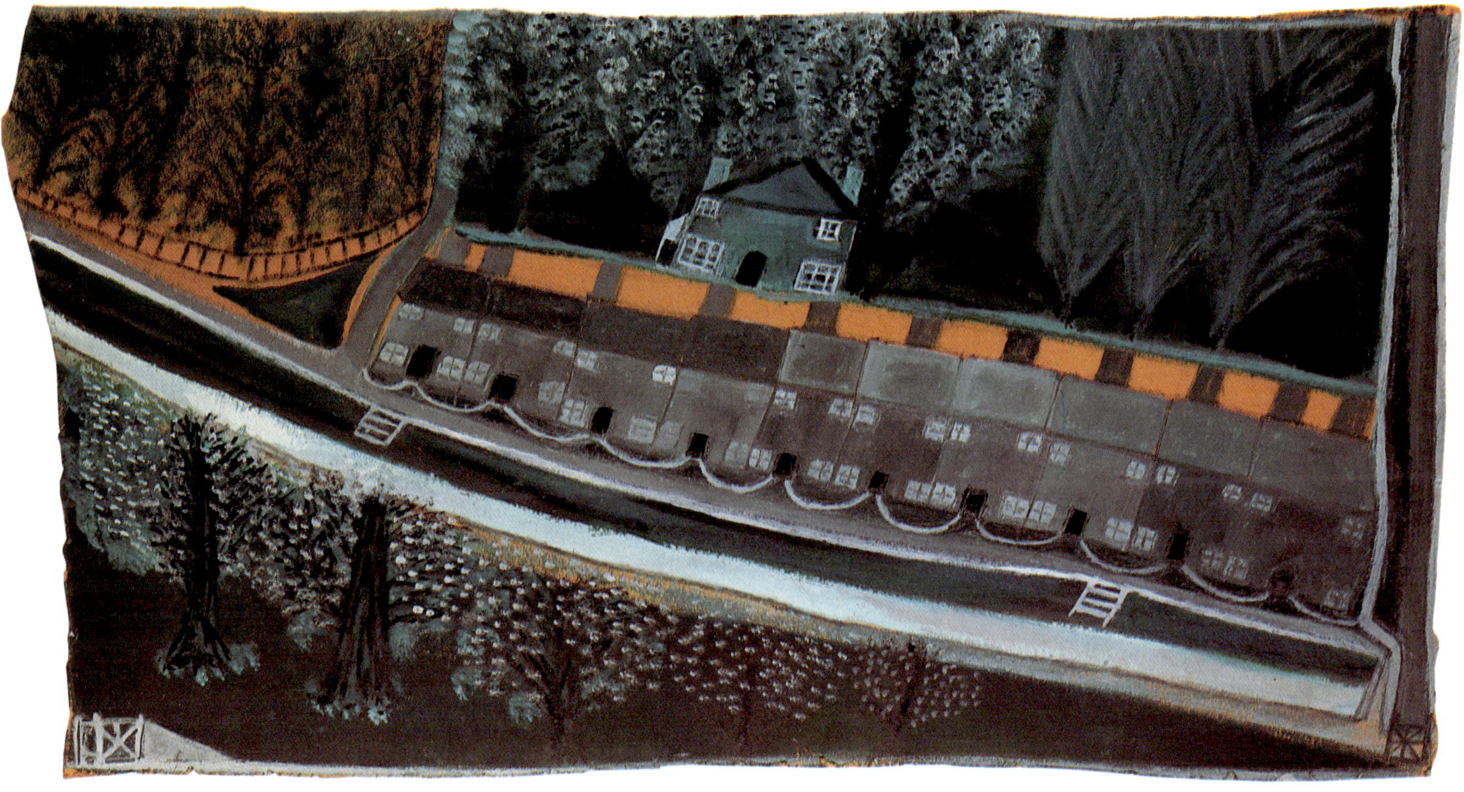

Houses and trees

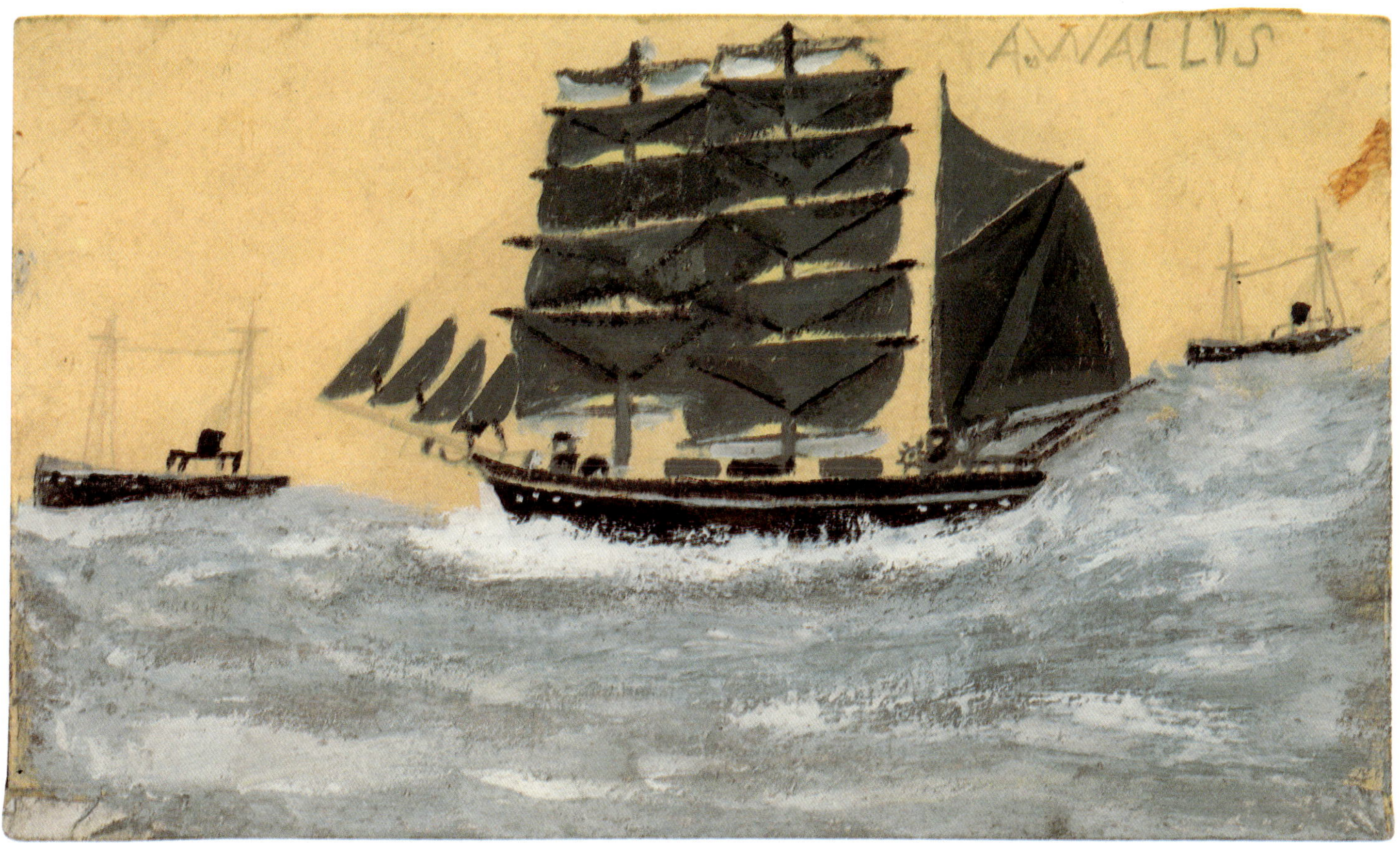

Sailing ship on a grey sea

RIGHT *Lighthouse and ships.*
Wallis liked to paint on the flat
surface of his table (see p. 18),
working from more than one side,
hence the angle of the right-hand
boat

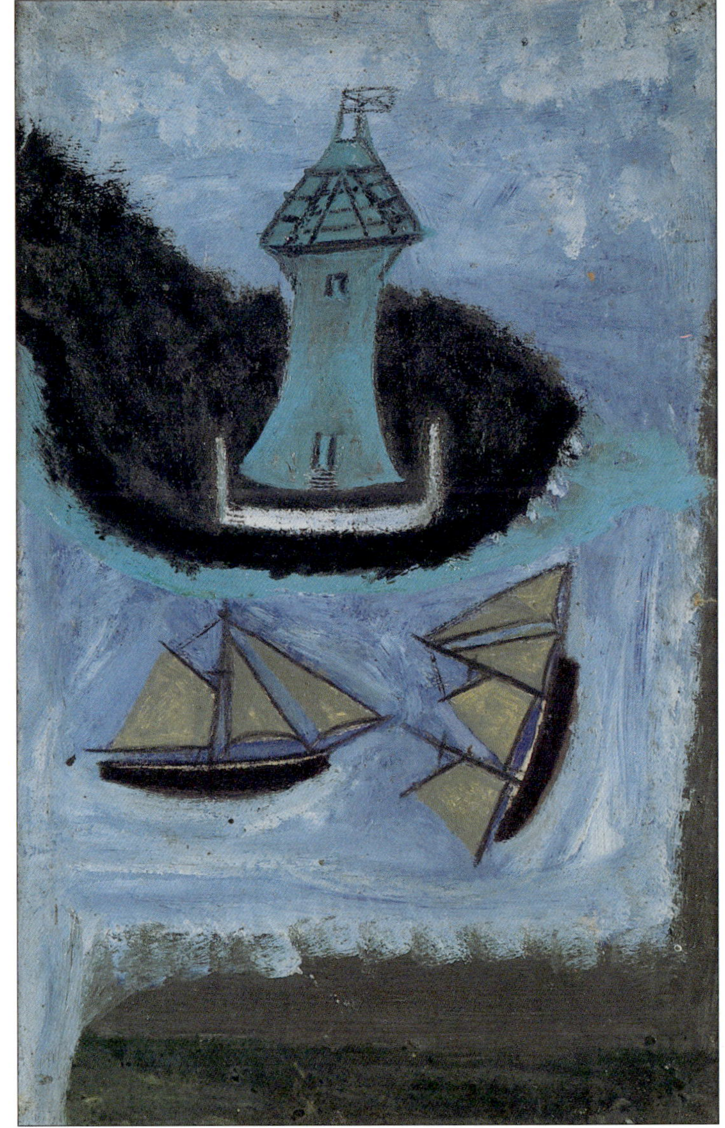

RIGHT *The blue ship, Mount's*
Bay. 'i thought it not nessery to
paint it all round so i never Don
it'. (Letter to H. S. Ede, 1929).
In the background is the artist's
stylised version of St. Michael's
Mount

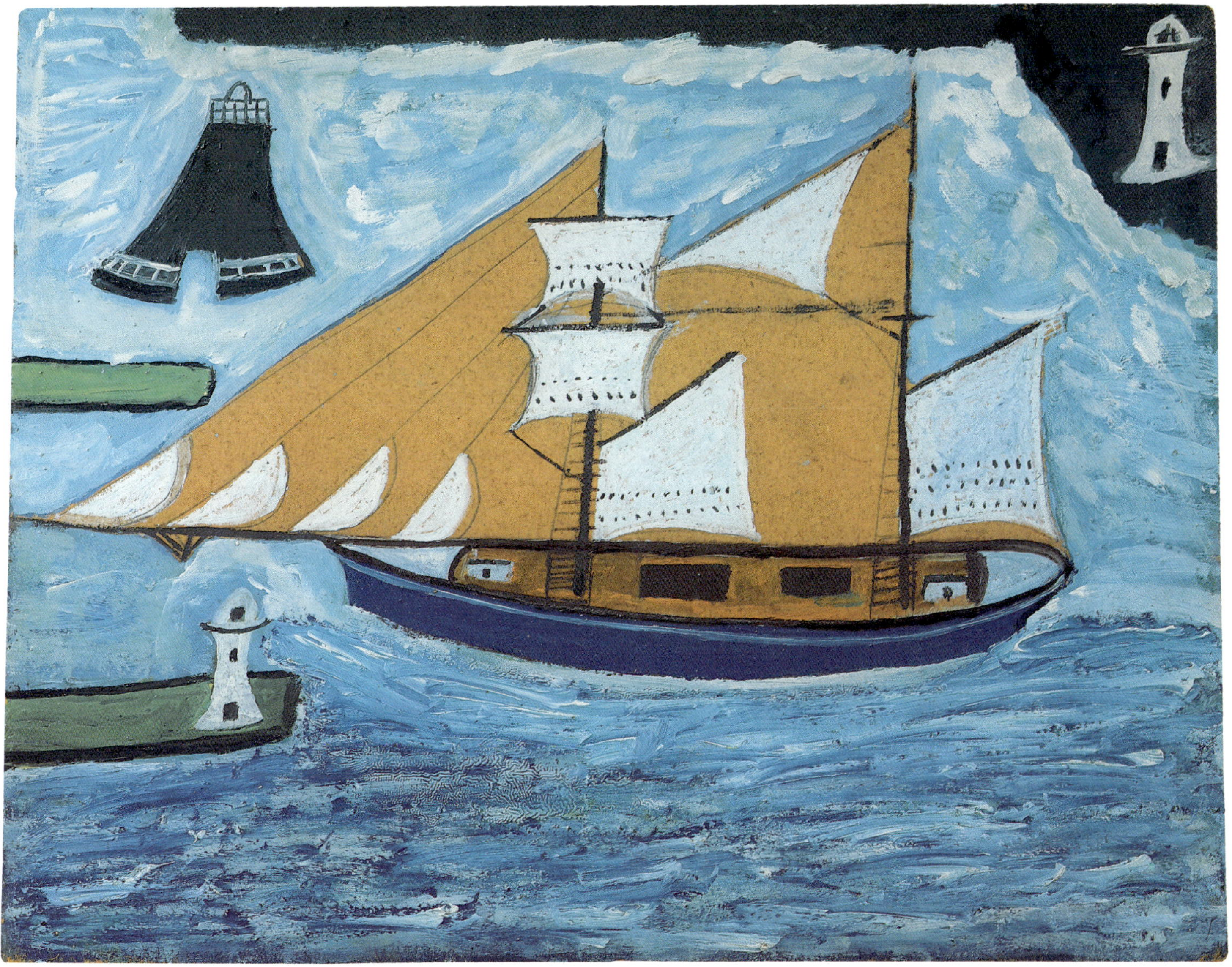

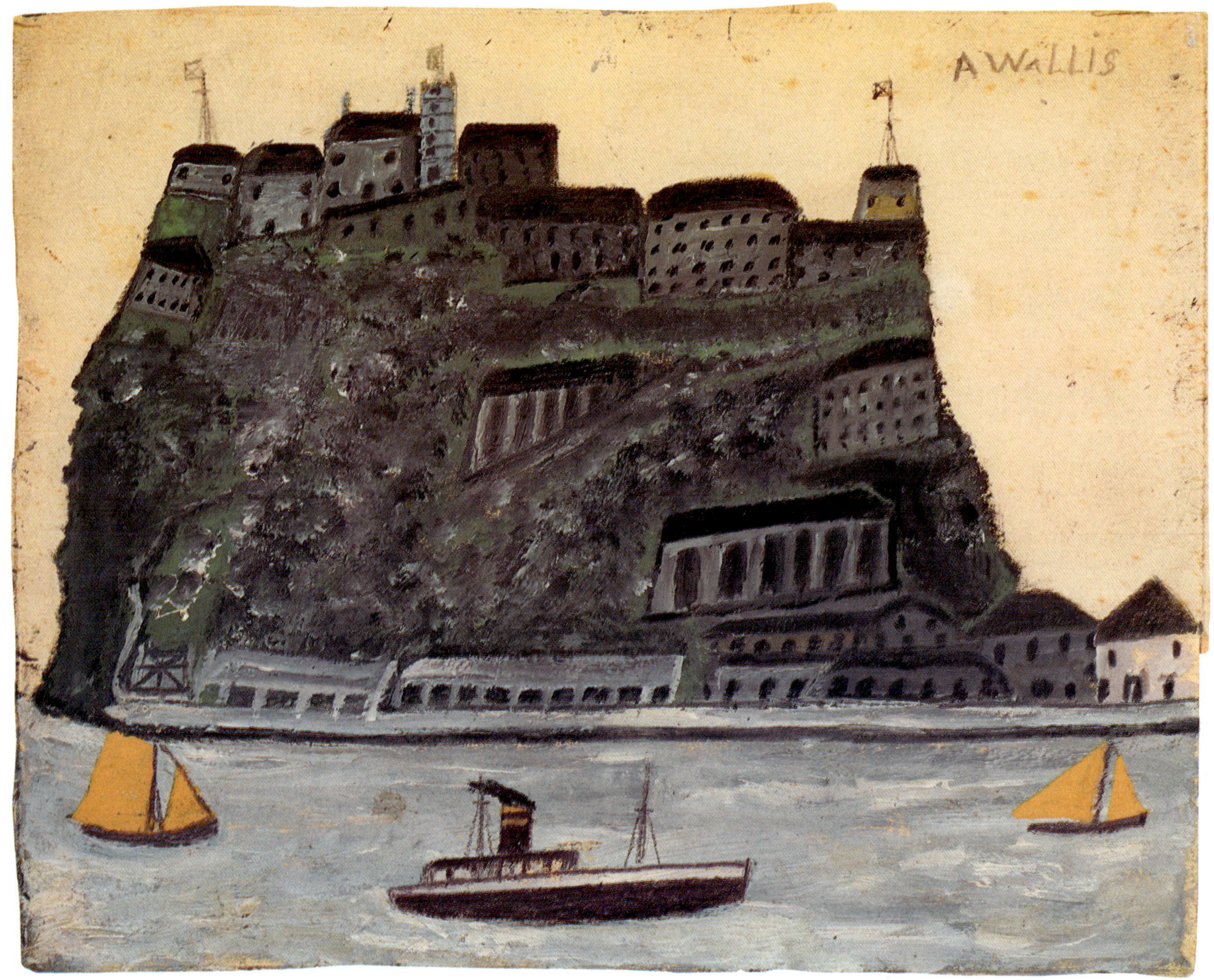

A WaLLiS

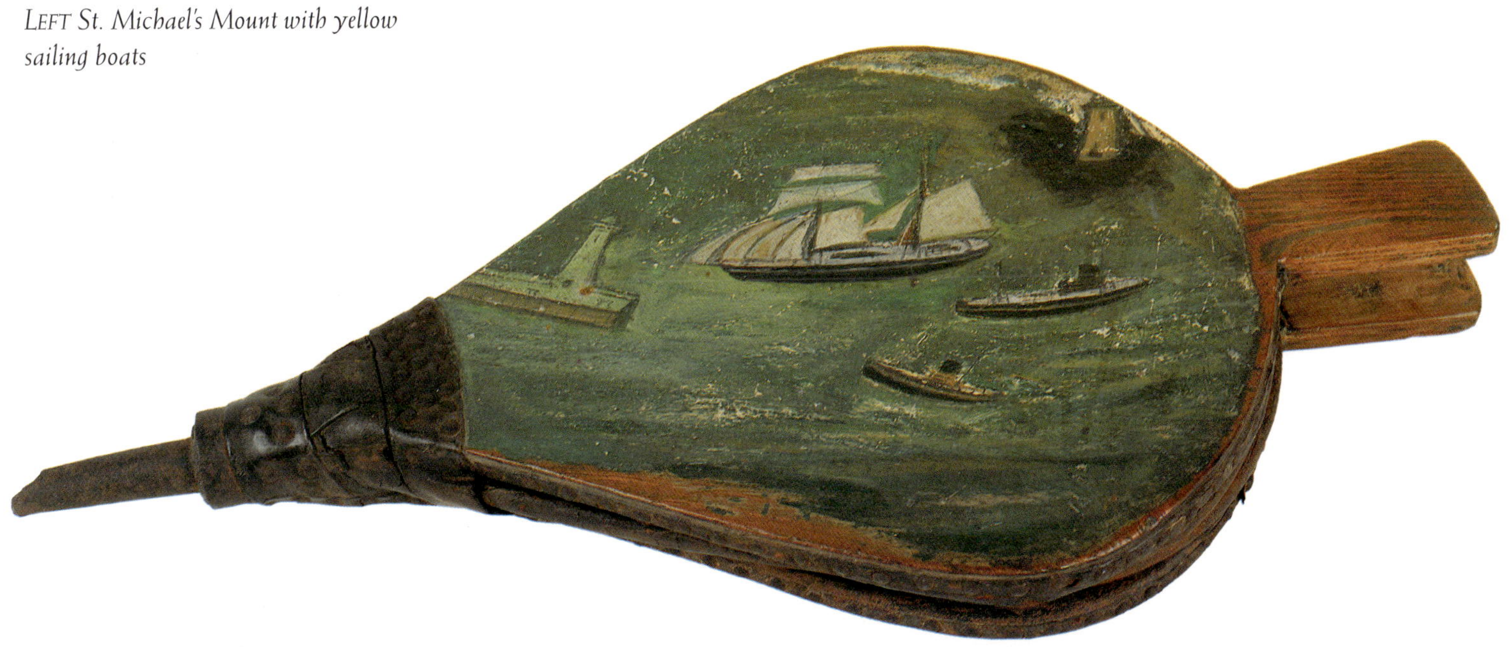

ABOVE St. Ives and Godrevy lighthouse – painted on a bellows. 'He used to
be forever painting . . . paint on anything that you gave him . . . nothing was
safe from where paint could go like.' (George Farrell in a tape-recording made by
Dr. Roger Slack, see p. 9–15)

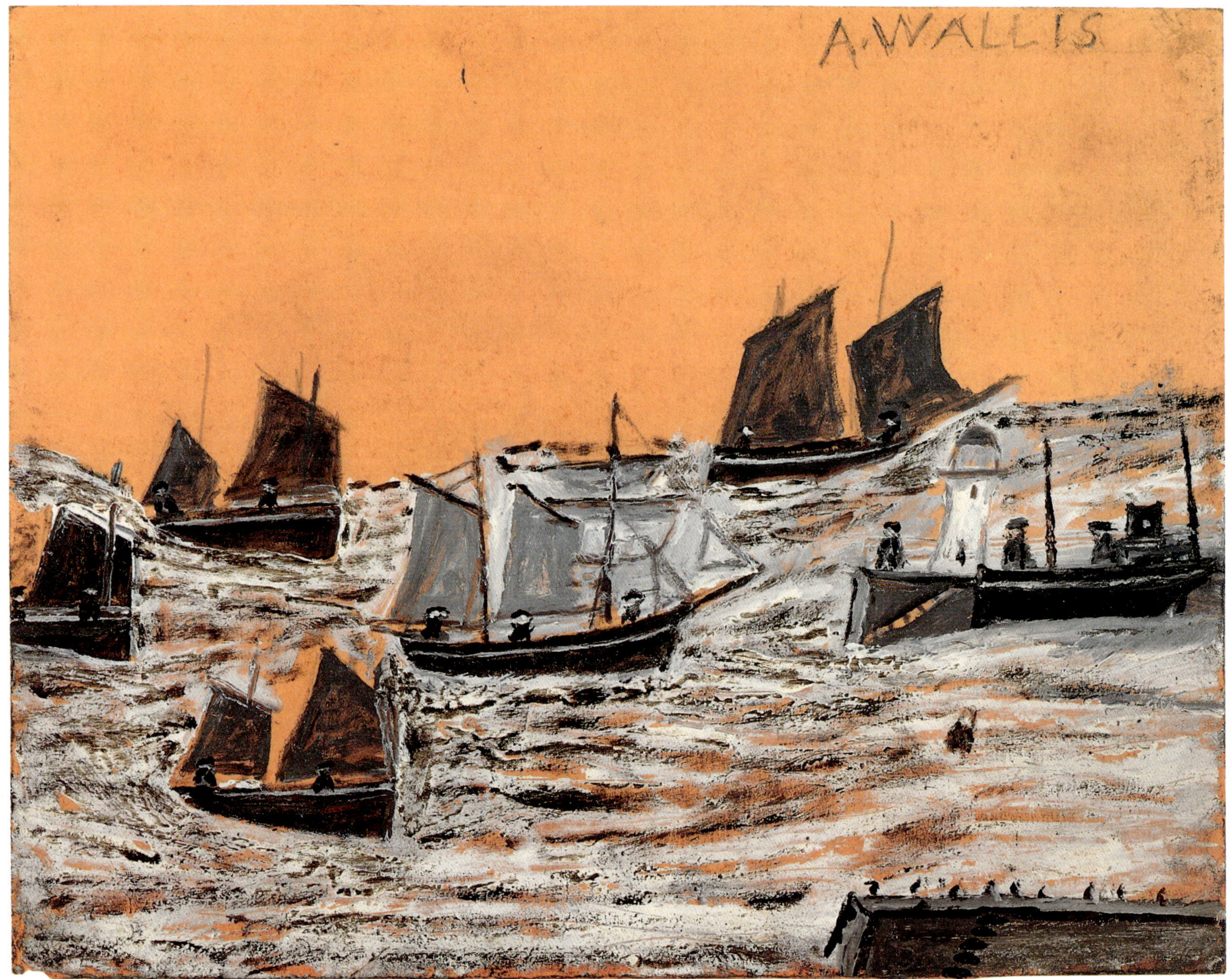

Sailing boats entering harbour

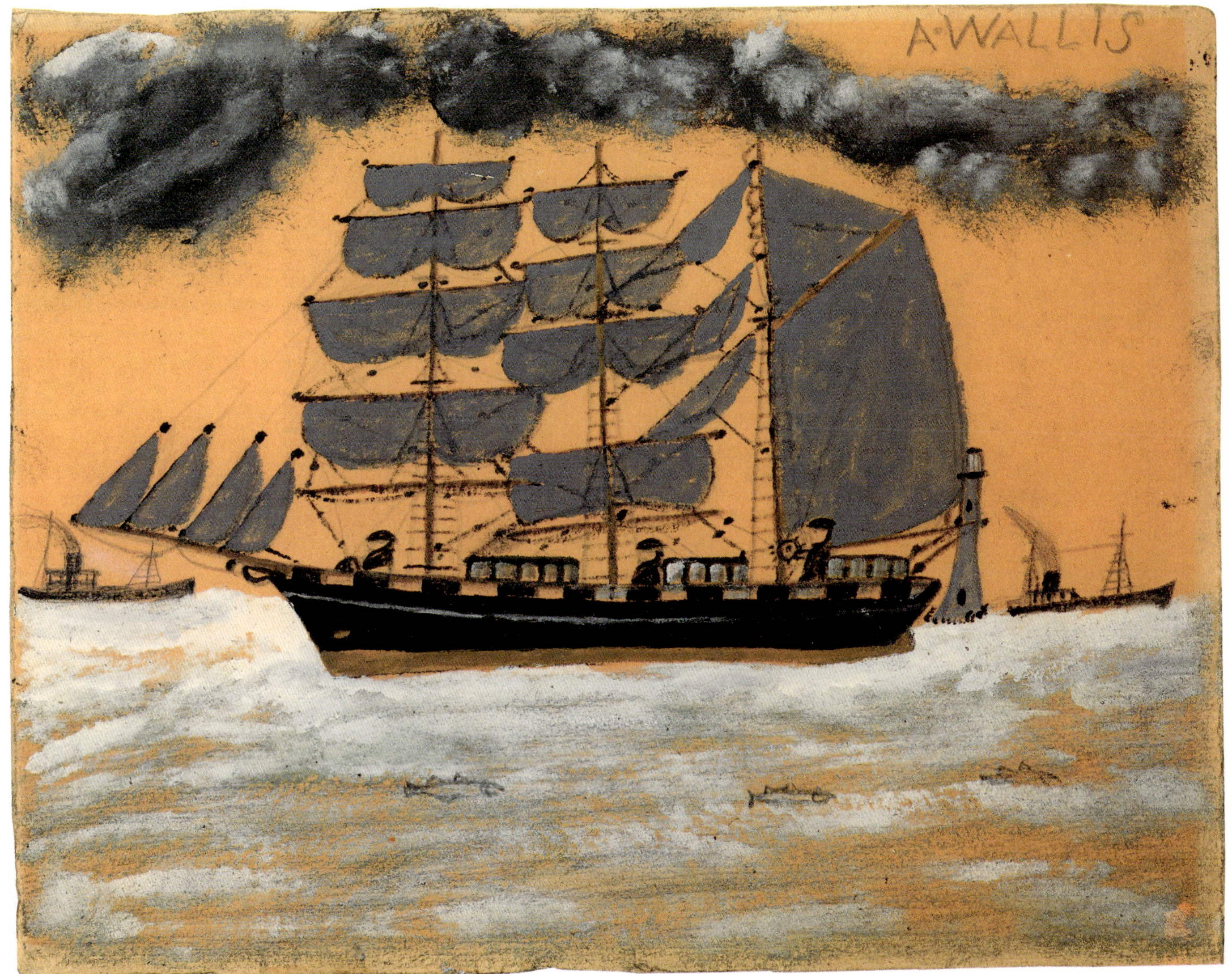

Three-master passing a lighthouse

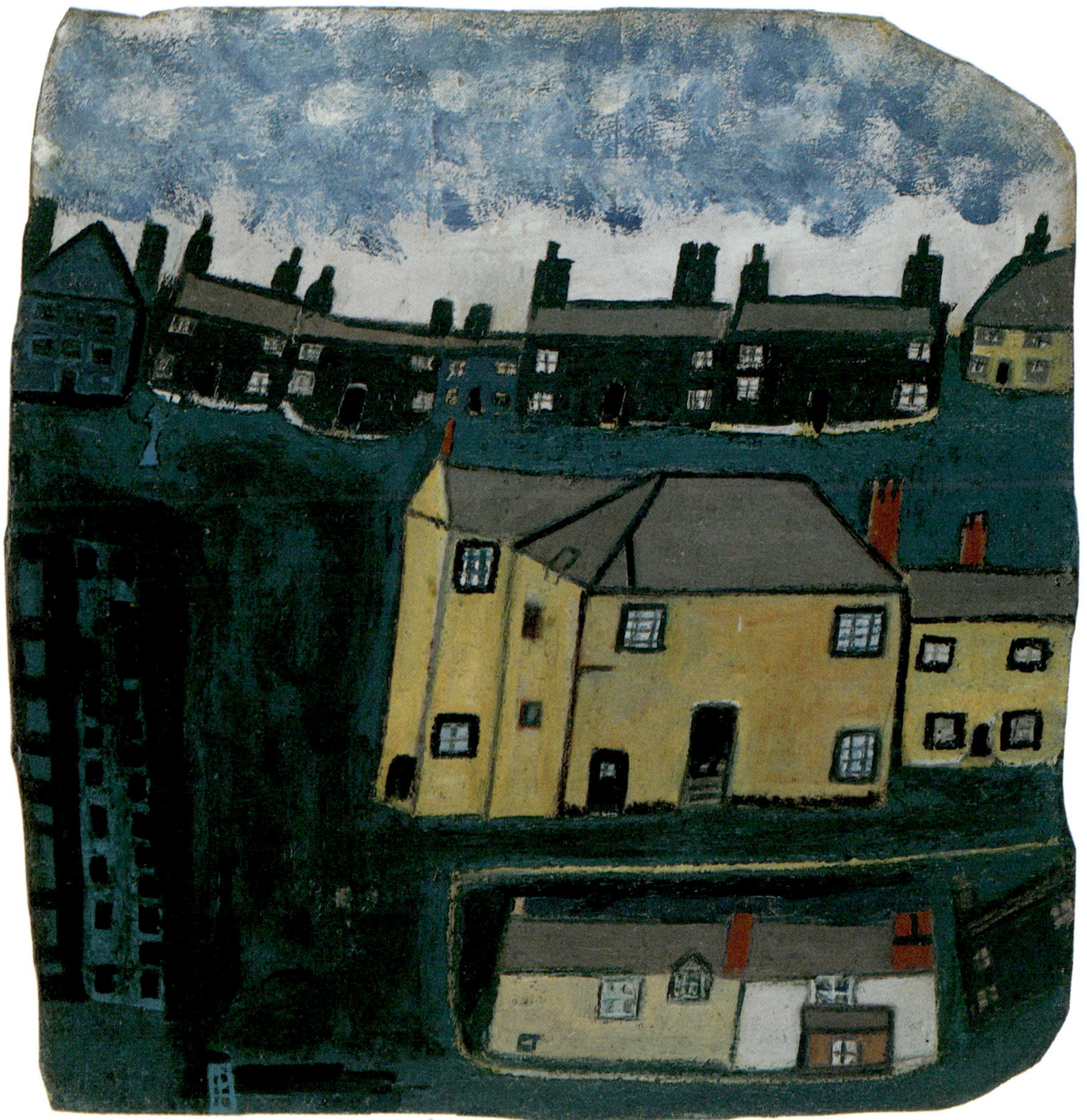

'Old House and Port Mear Square' (inscribed on the back). Dame Barbara Hepworth, who formerly owned the painting, remembered Wallis explaining that it represented 'St. Ives in the dark days'

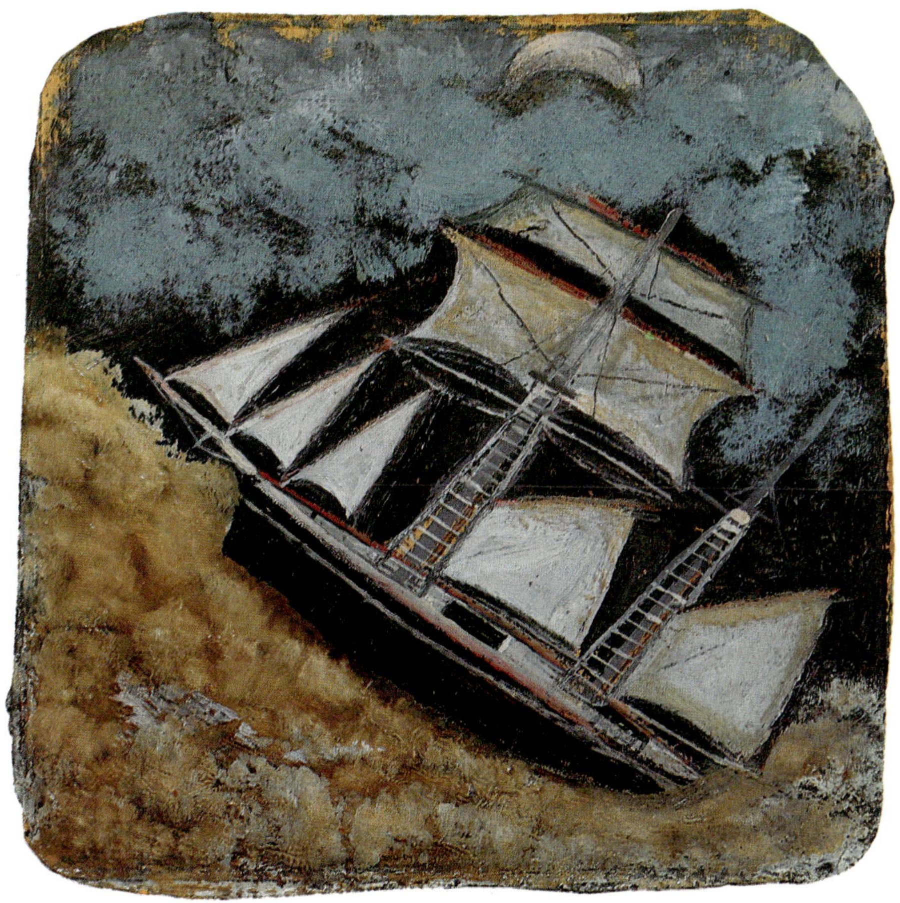

Schooner under the moon. The inverted segment of moon (or possibly setting sun)
is a recurring image in Wallis' painting, as is the 'ship-in-a-bottle' effect of the
schooner trapped between stormy sea and clouds

RIGHT The wreck of the Alba and lighthouse. On 31 January 1938, the Panamanian steamer Alba with a cargo of coal ran aground in heavy seas off Porthmeor Beach. The St. Ives lifeboat was launched, but capsized in the storm, and five crewmen were drowned. Wallis probably witnessed the event, and made a number of paintings of it

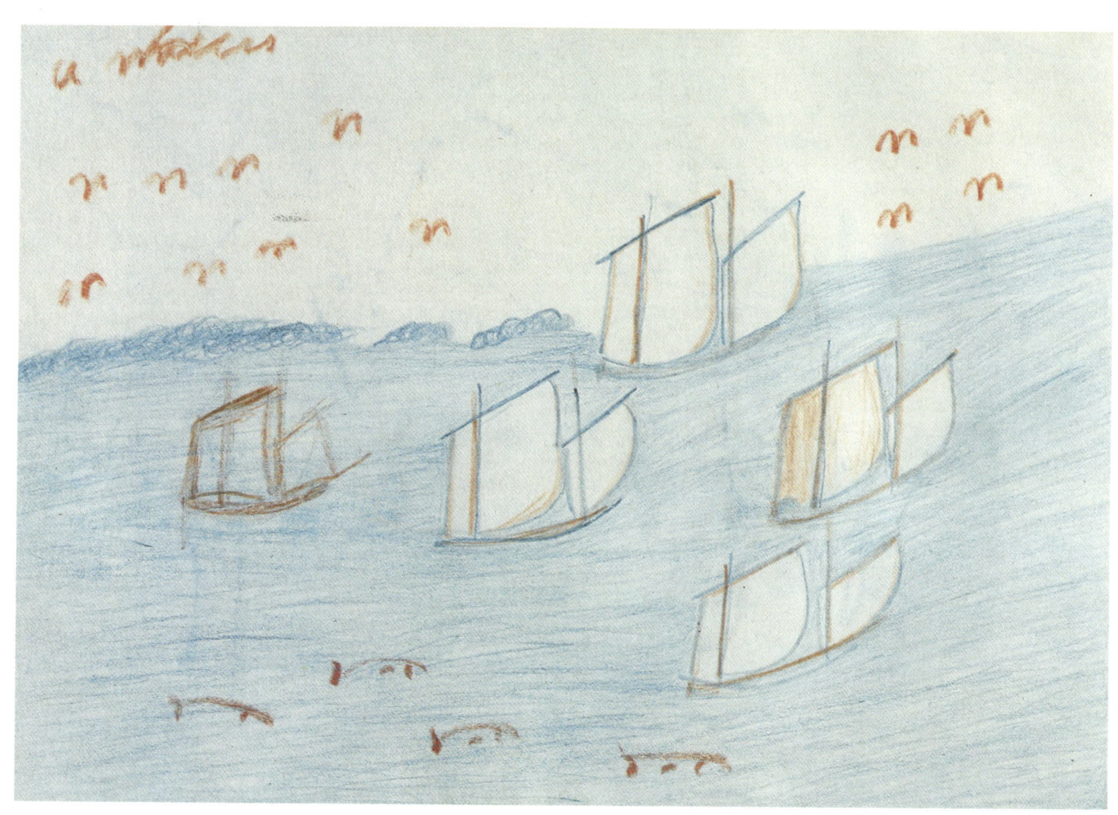

ABOVE Sailing boats with fishes and birds. Wallis filled many sketchbooks with crayon drawings, particularly late in his life and in the workhouse when he could not always obtain his favourite ships' oil paint

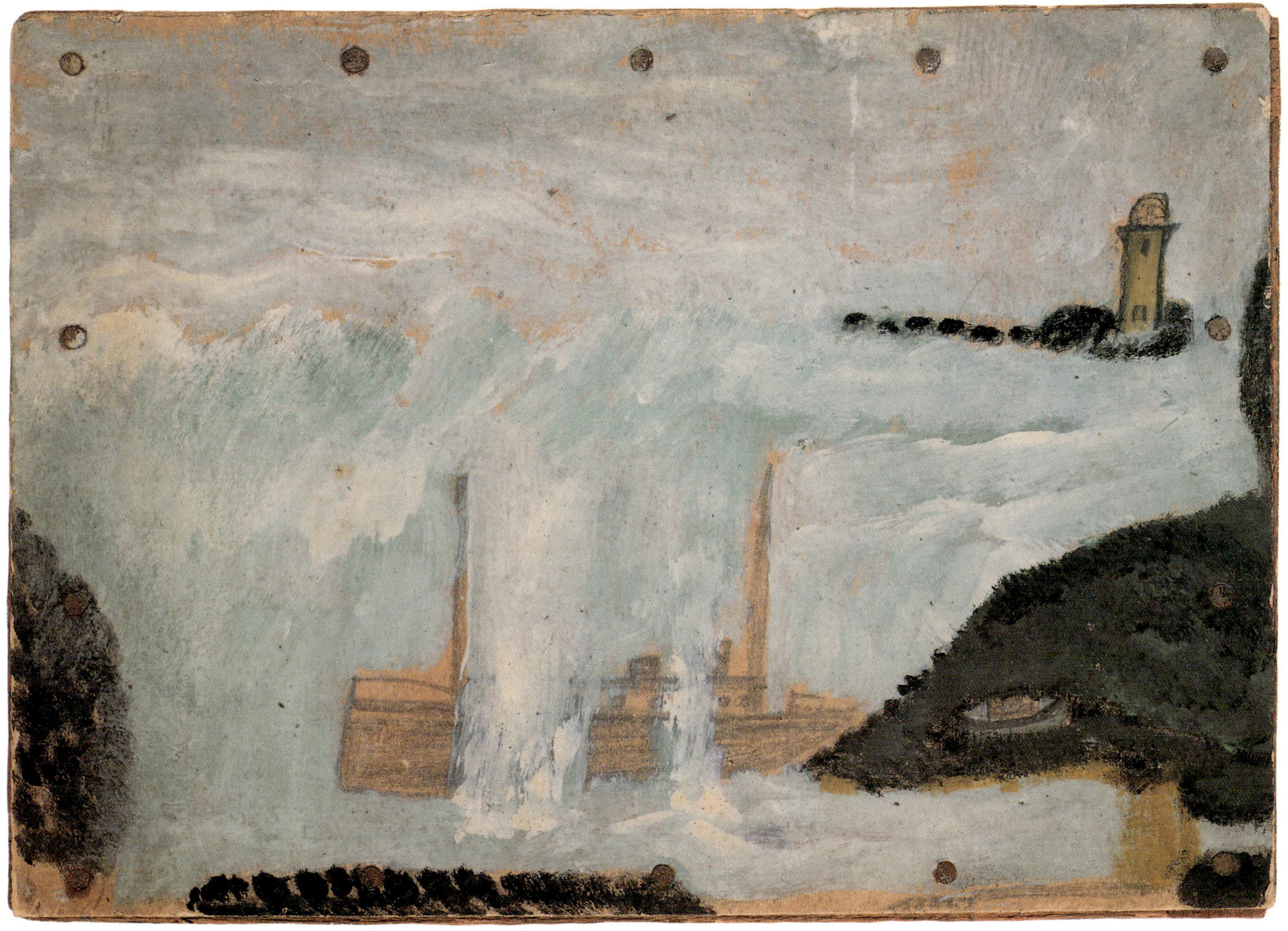

RIGHT Houses with gateway

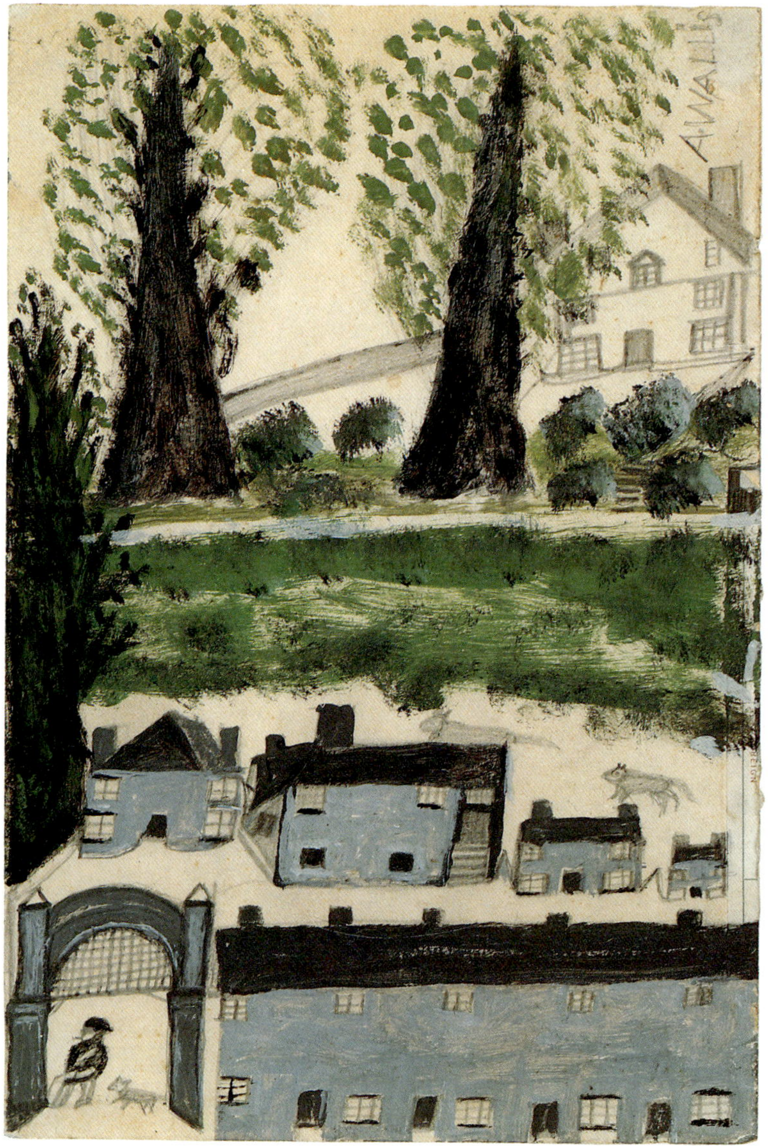

RIGHT Yacht, pink and green

*OVERLEAF Three-master in full
sail, with a lighthouse*

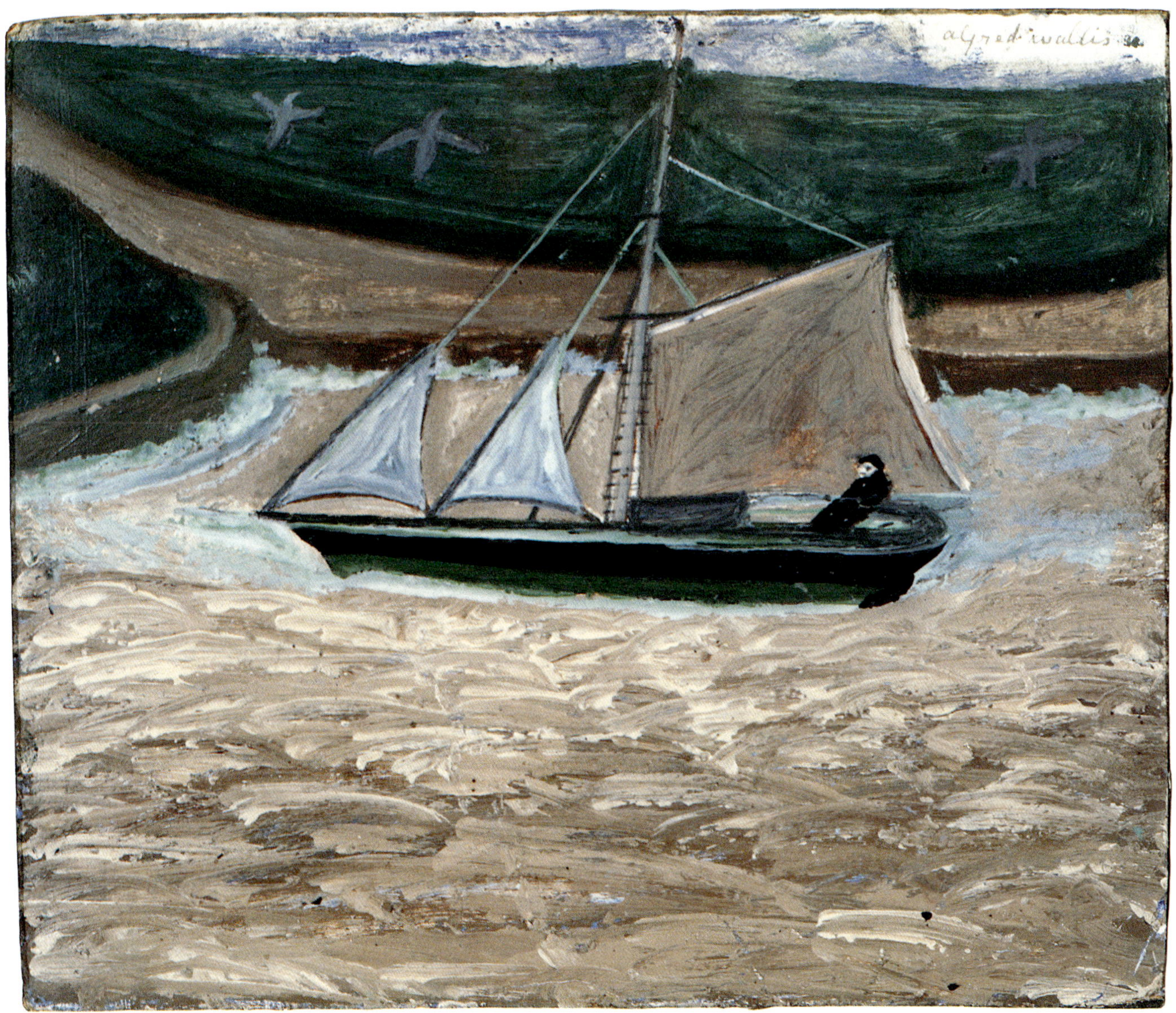

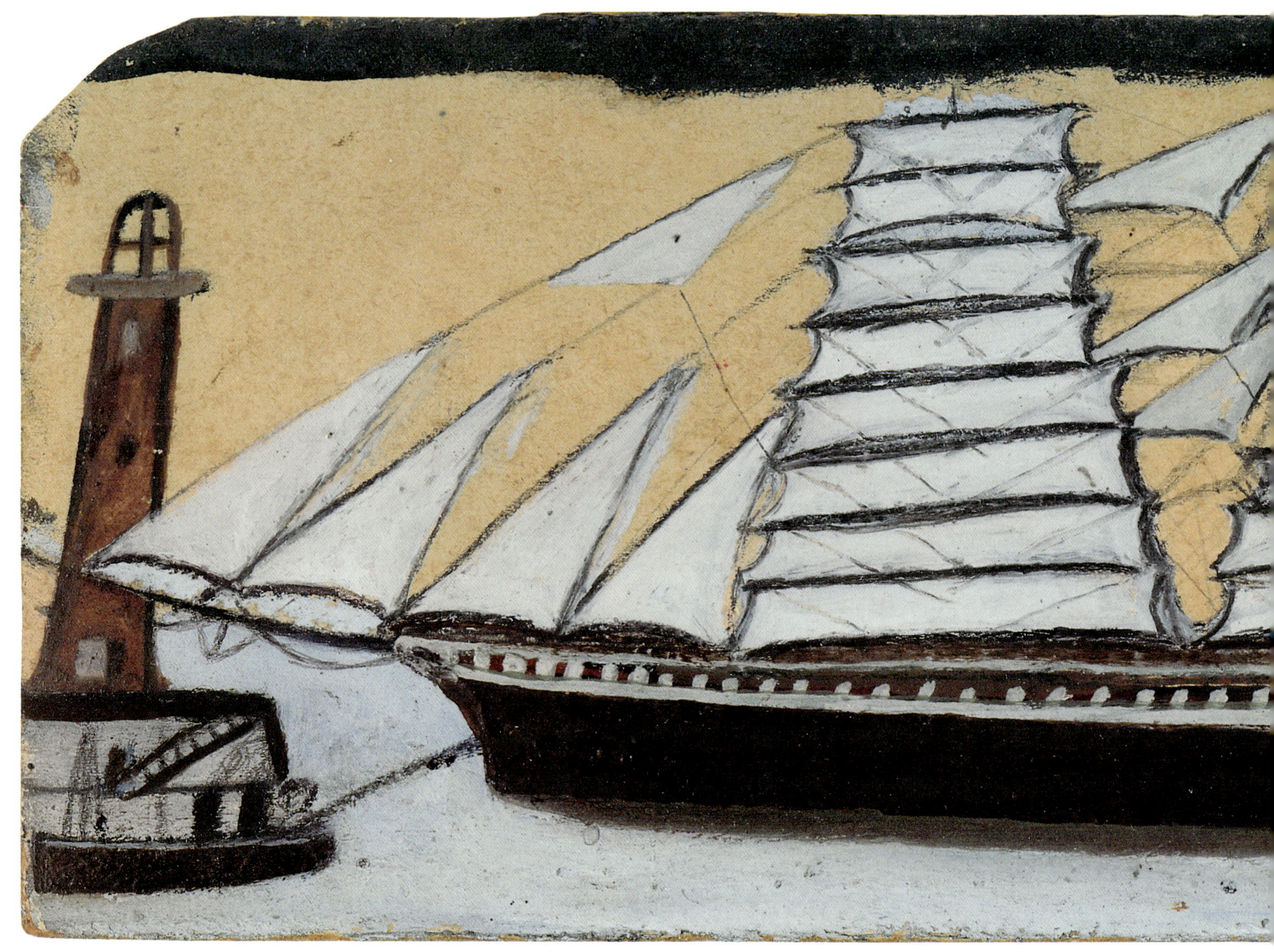

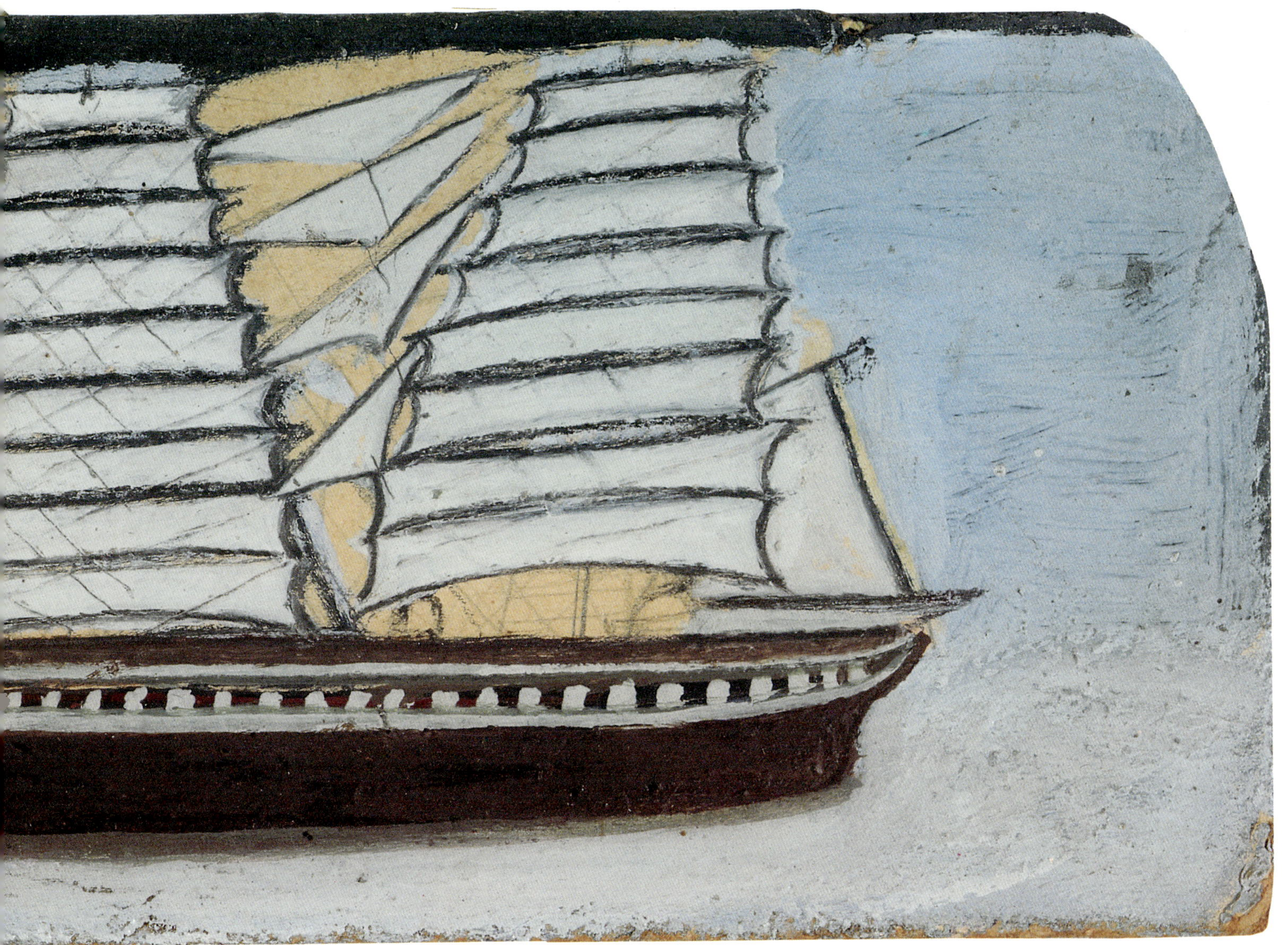

BELOW Two steamers in St. Ives Bay

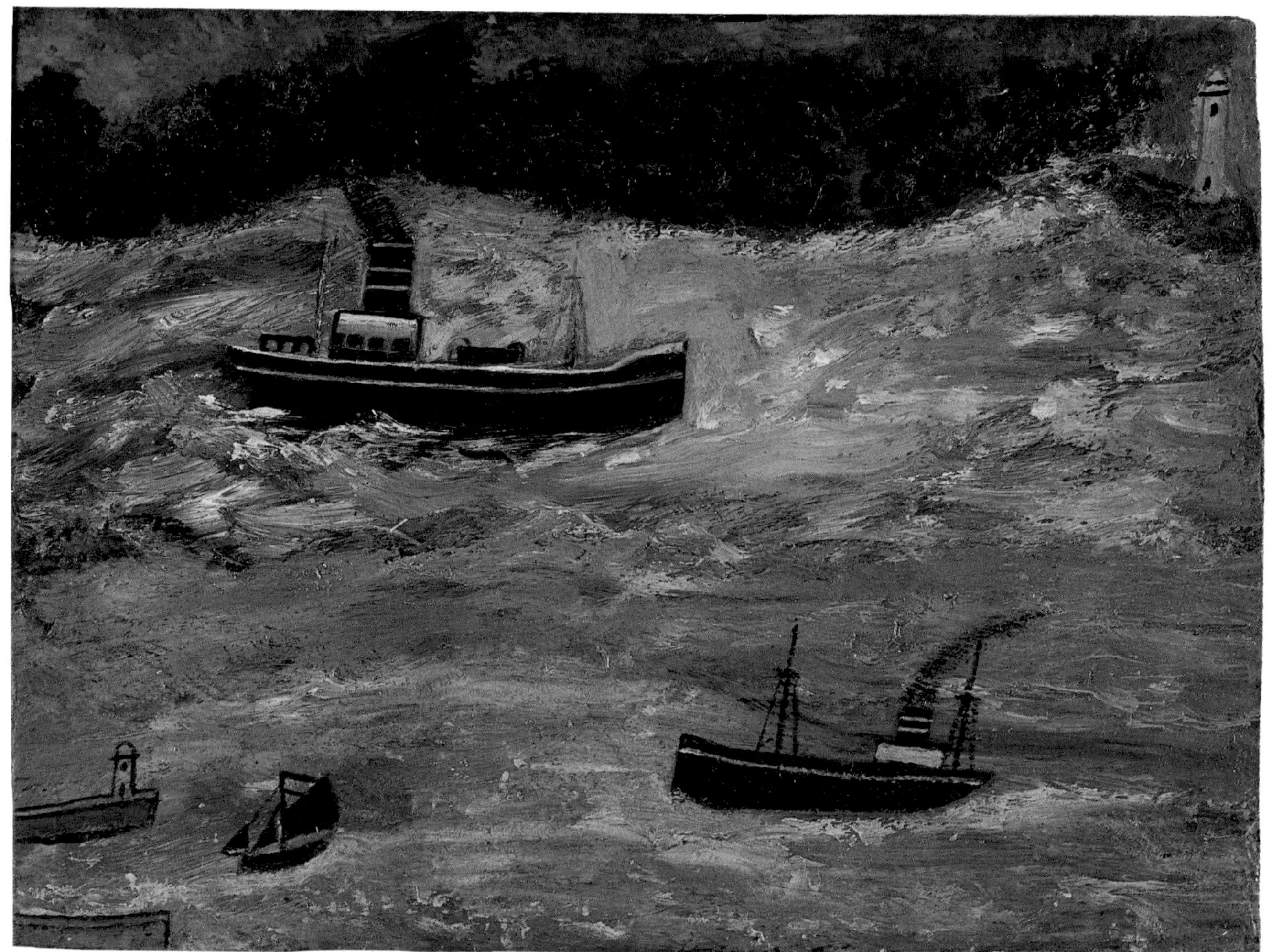

RIGHT Schooner

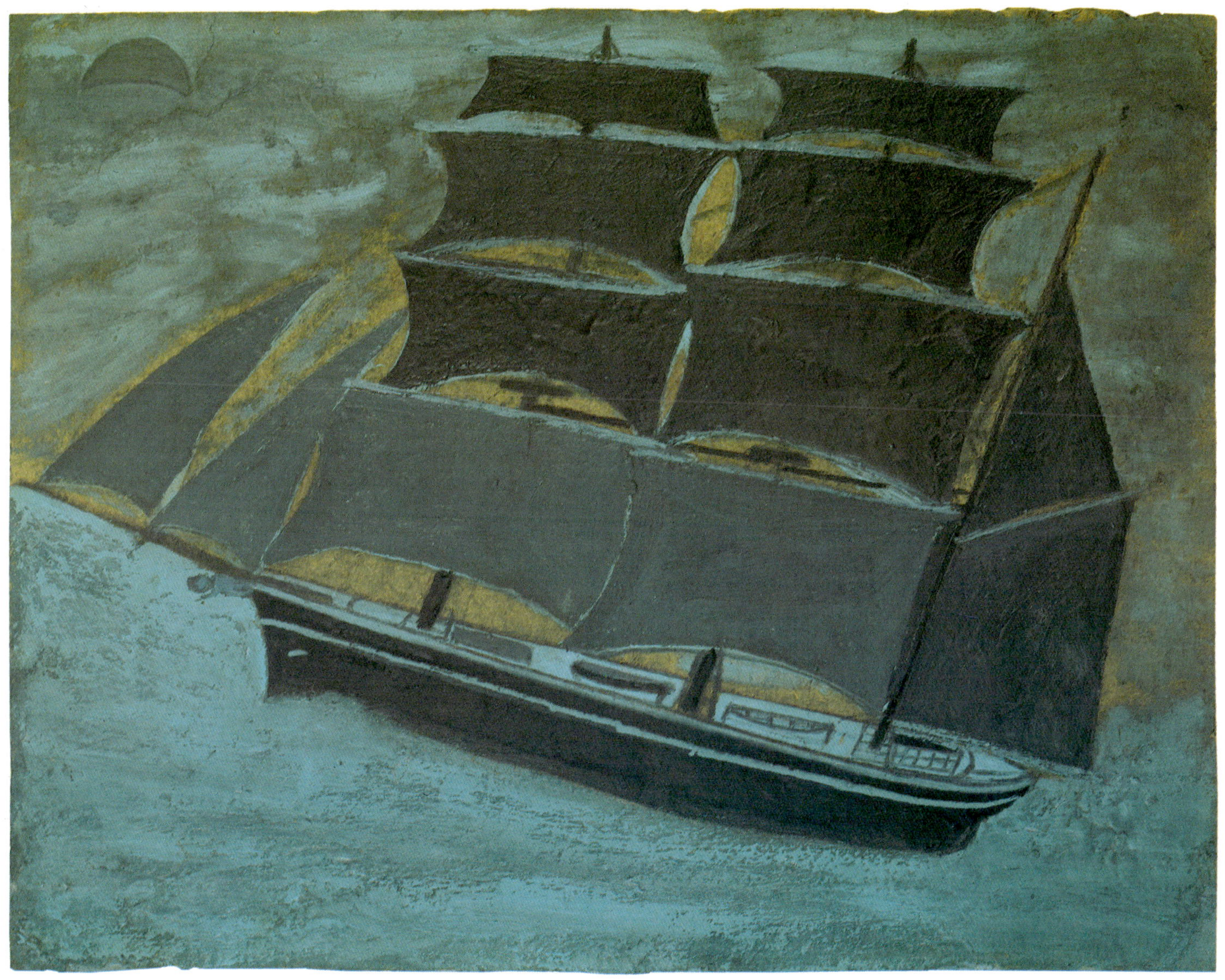

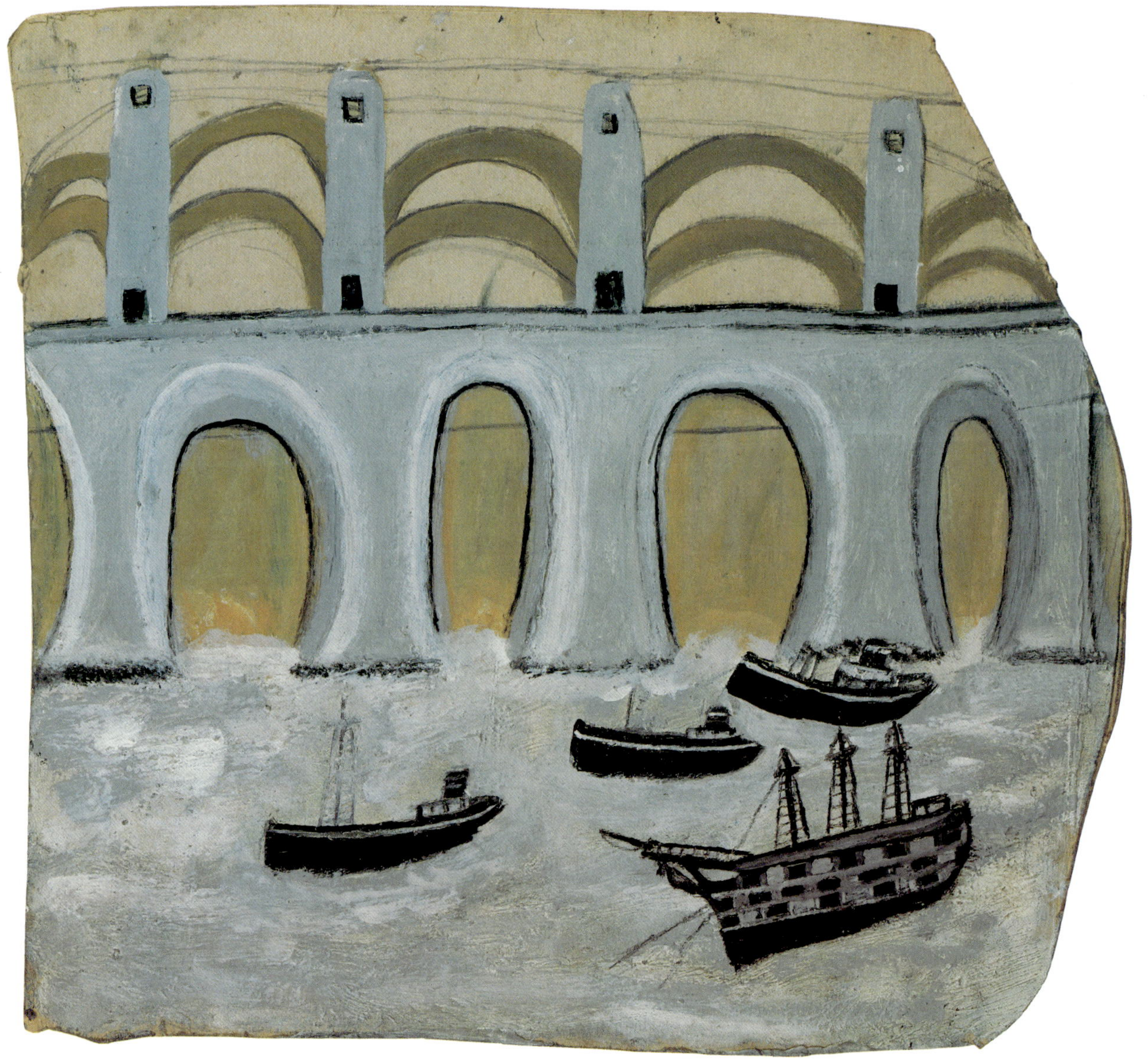

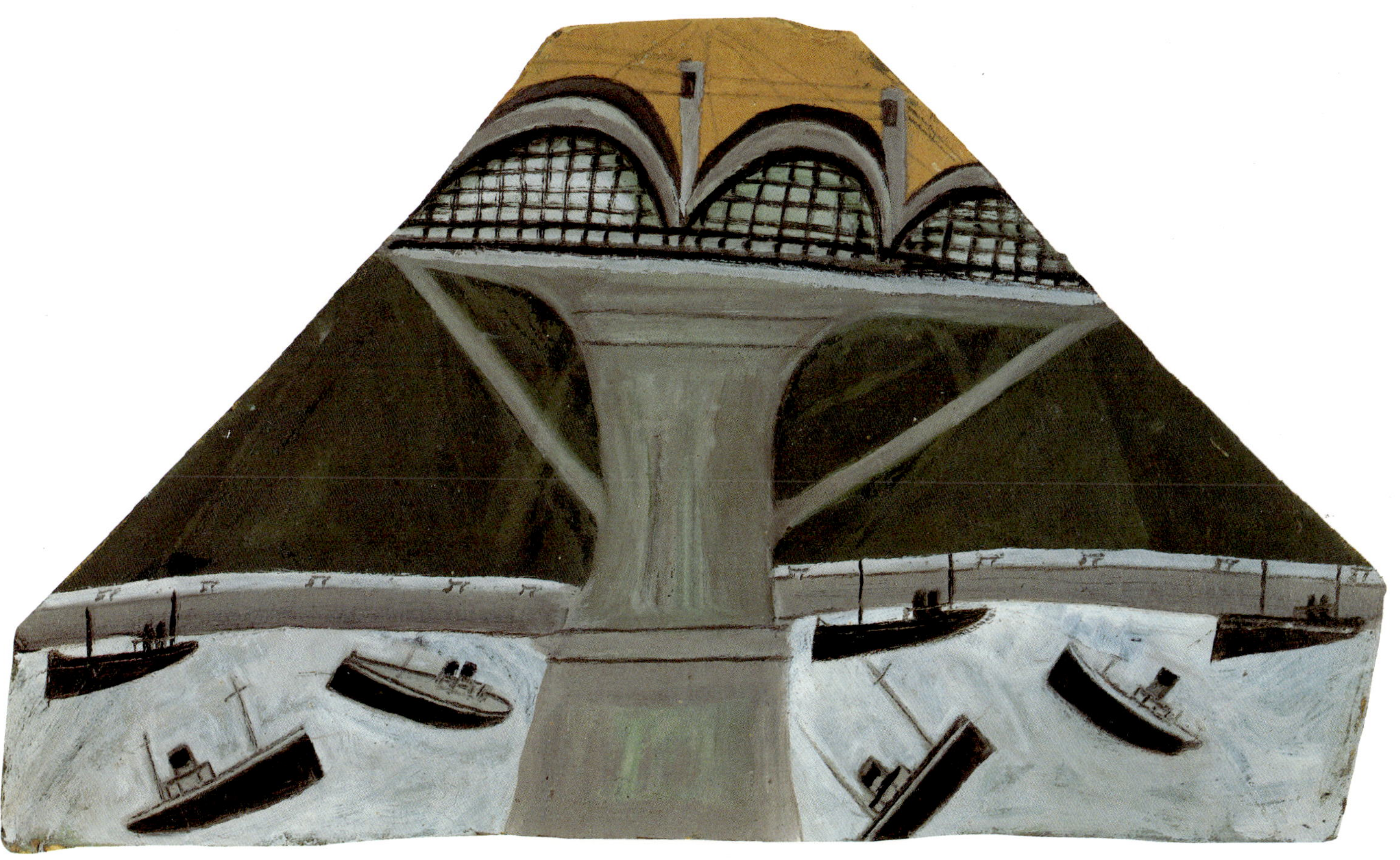

LEFT *Saltash Bridge and training ship. Wallis had been a small boy in Devonport when I. K. Brunel's road-and-railway bridge over the River Tamar was completed in 1859. Recollected from early childhood, the curious shapes of this massive tubular construction recur in a number of Wallis' paintings*

ABOVE *Saltash Bridge. Brunel's great bridge, with one of its huge supports, has here been made into a kind of capstone, with boats tossing in the harbour beneath – an example of Wallis' imaginative use of an irregular-shaped board*

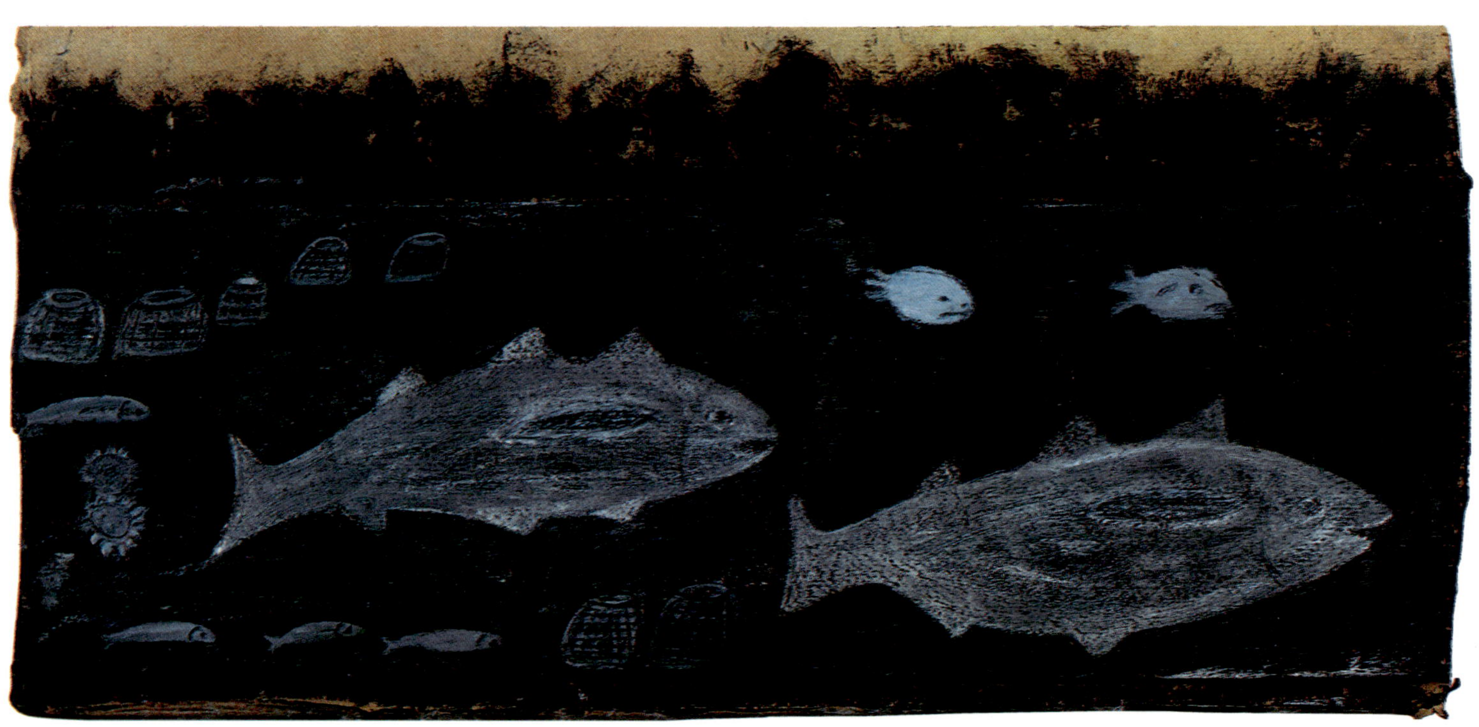

Fishes and lobster-pots

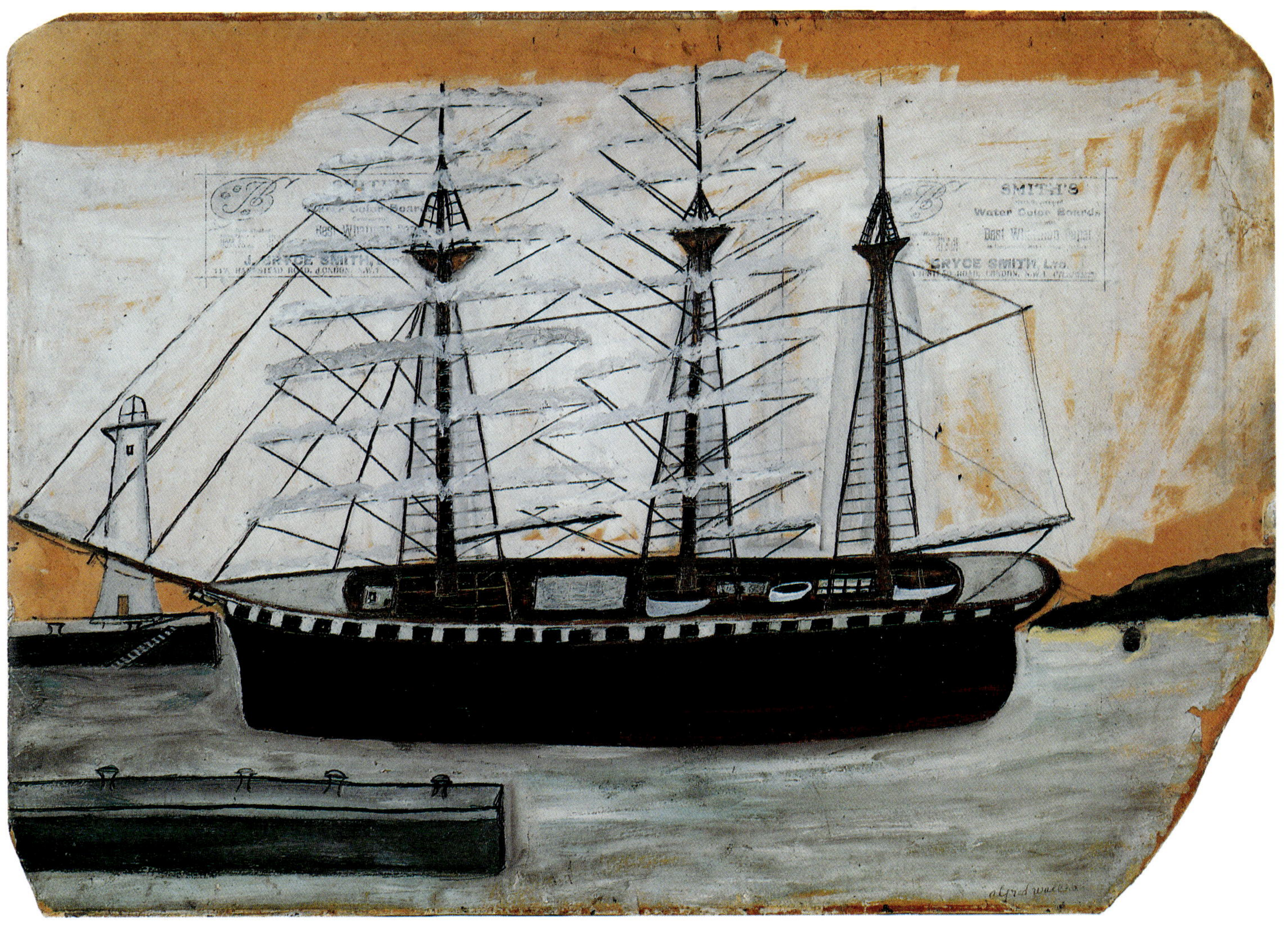

Three-master. Painted on a fragment of artists' watercolour board, doubtless given
to Wallis as scrap

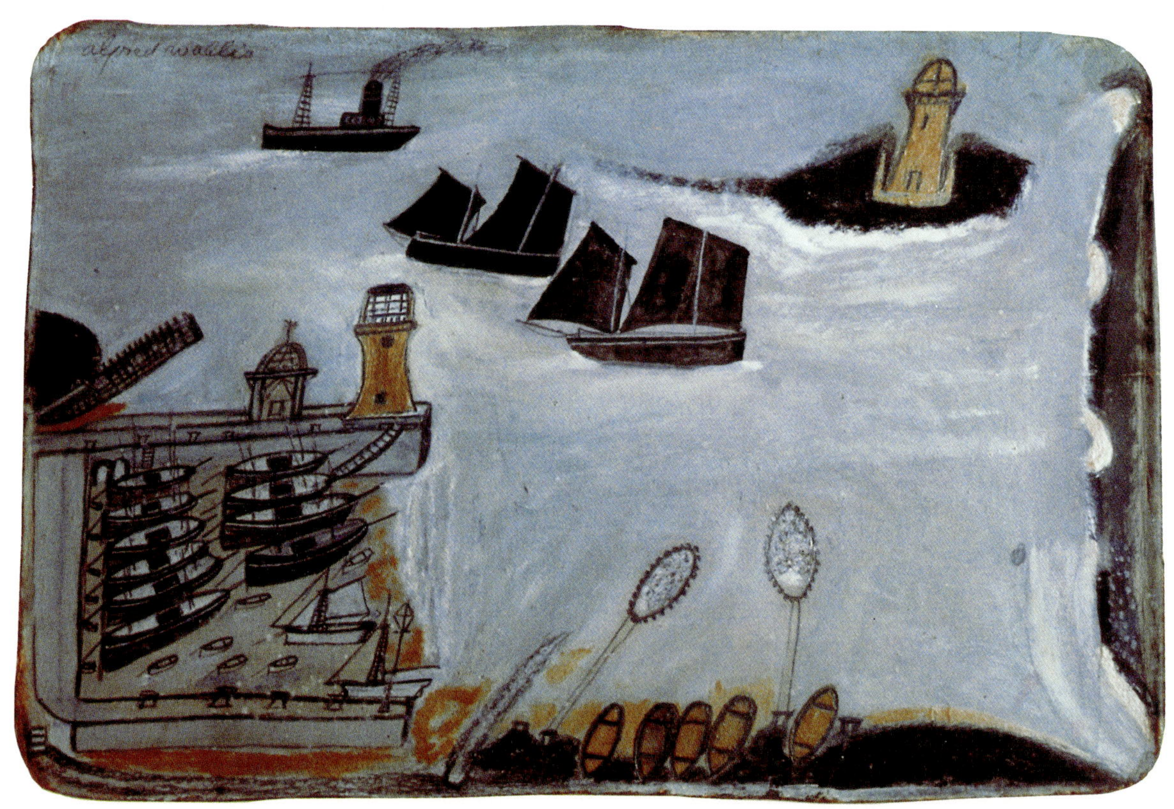

St. Ives harbour and Godrevy. Wallis' bird's-eye view pulls in the distant coastline and Godrevy lighthouse, as well as showing the 'seine' nets used for catching shoals of pilchards off Porthminster Beach

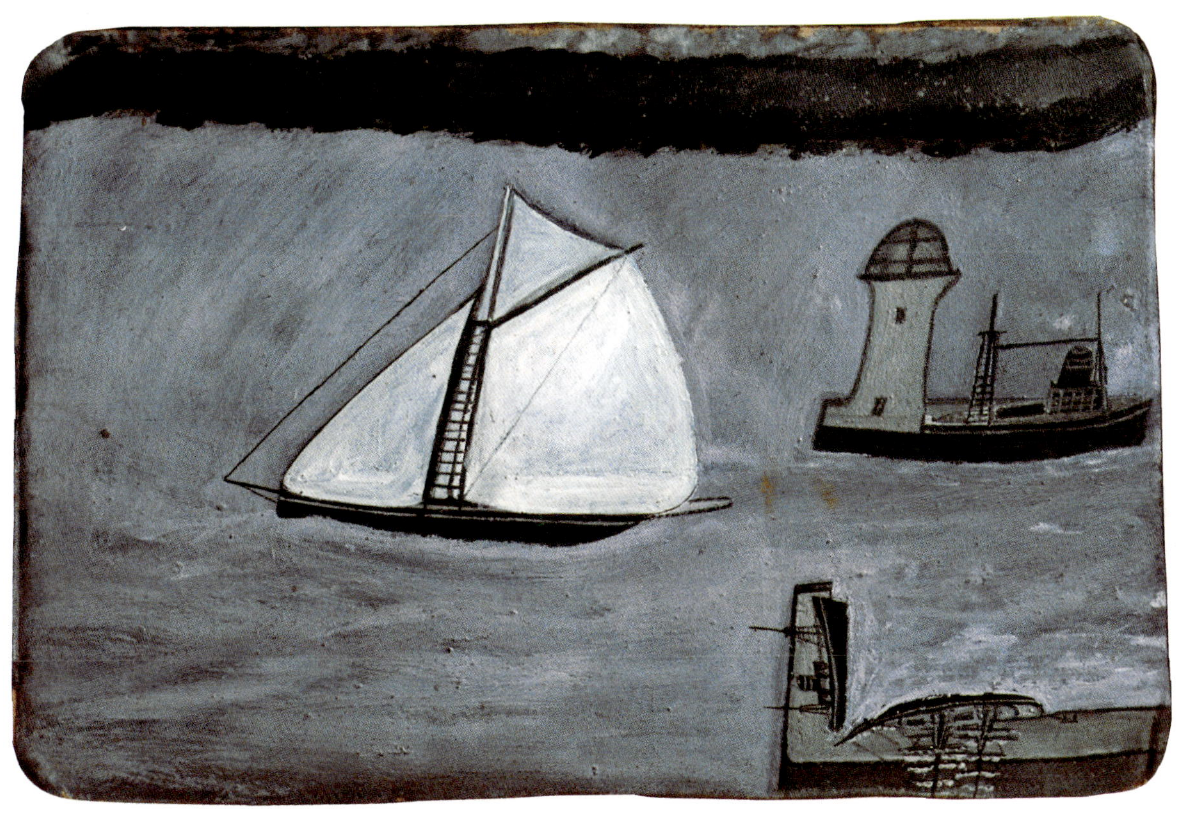

St. Ives harbour: white sailing ship. Wallis habitually worked on a flat table-top
adding images as he moved around it

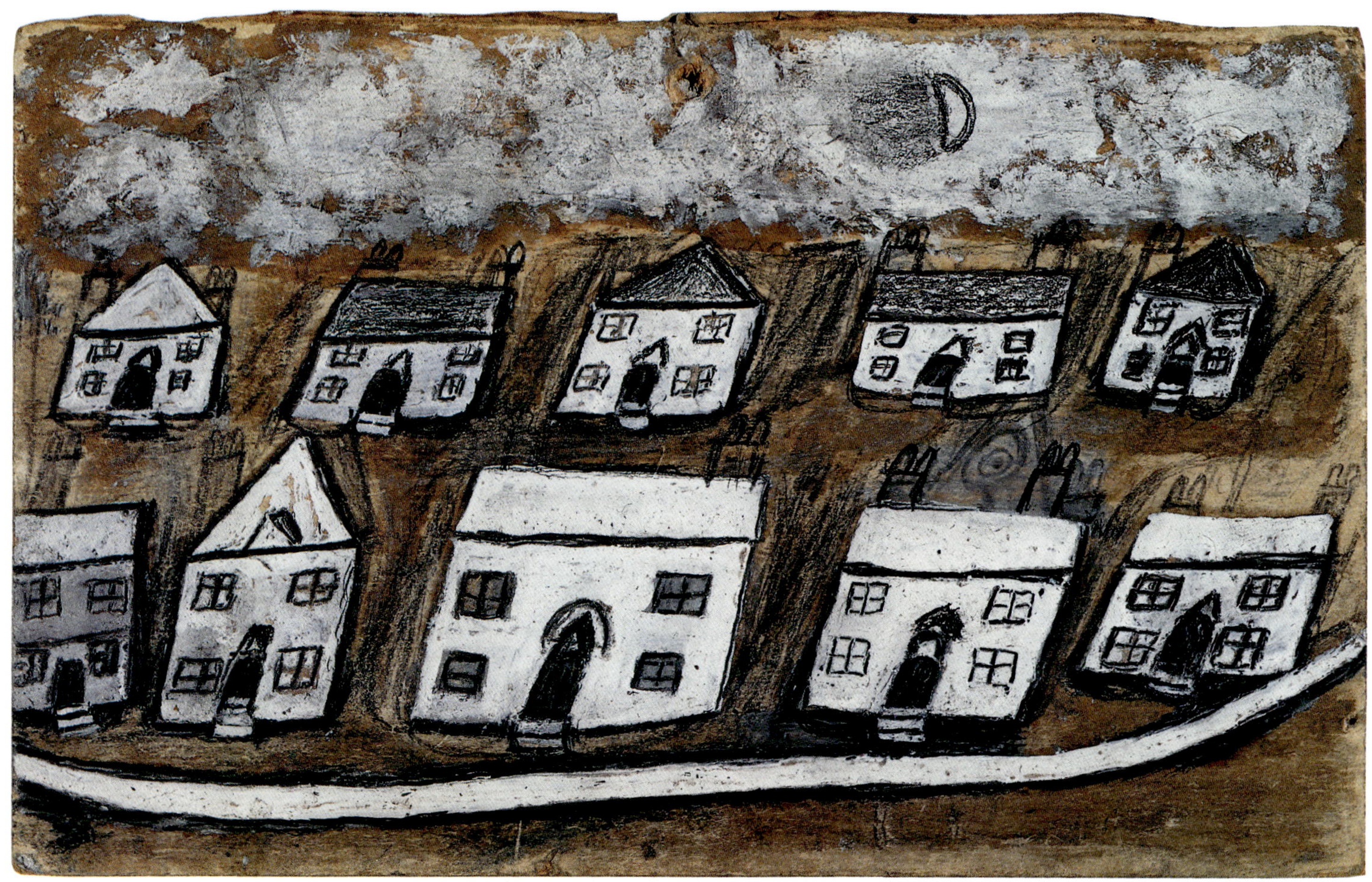

ABOVE *White houses*

RIGHT *Three-master with sea birds. Wallis painted on any material he could get hold of, in this case on an old blotter with red leather corners*

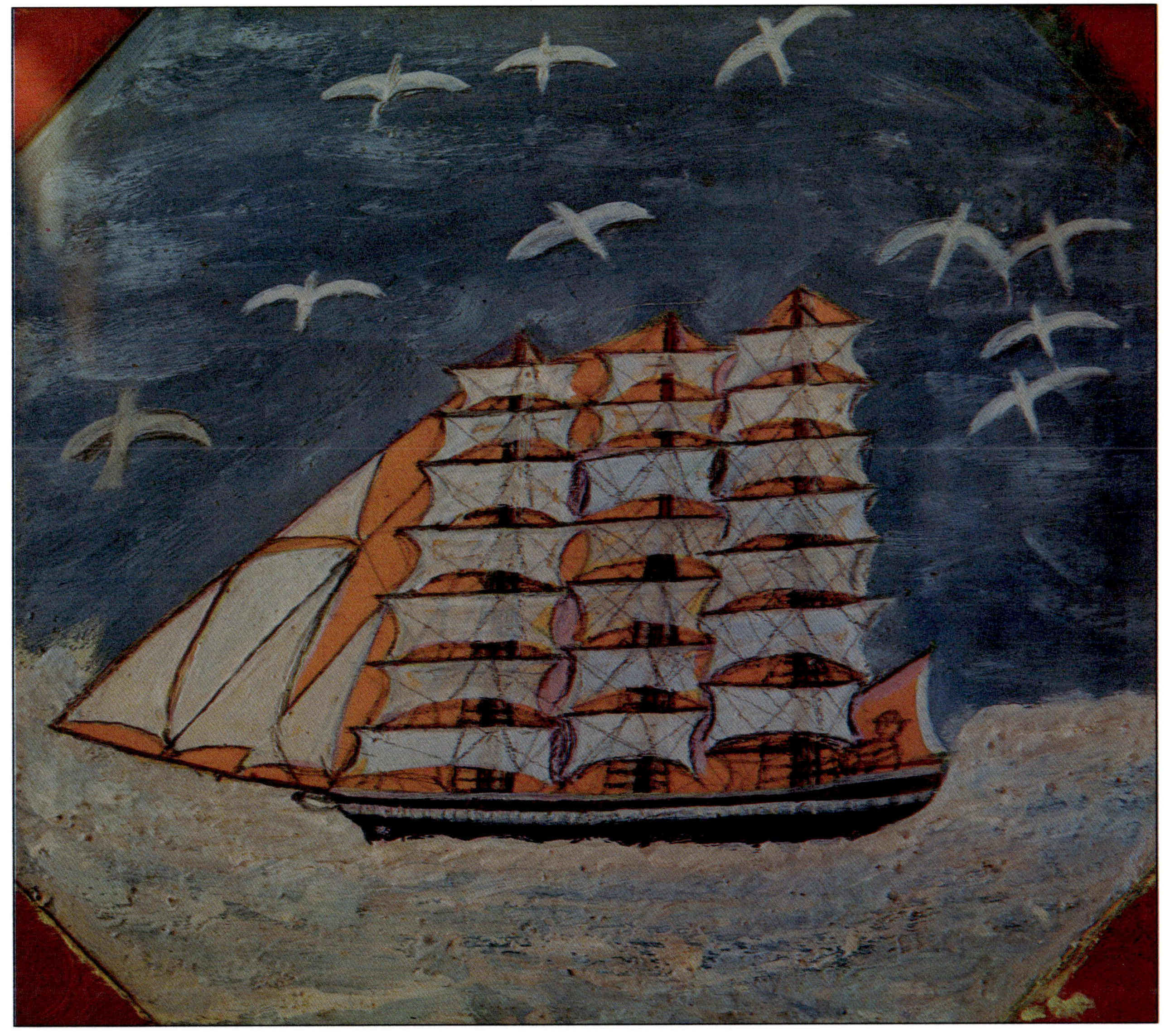

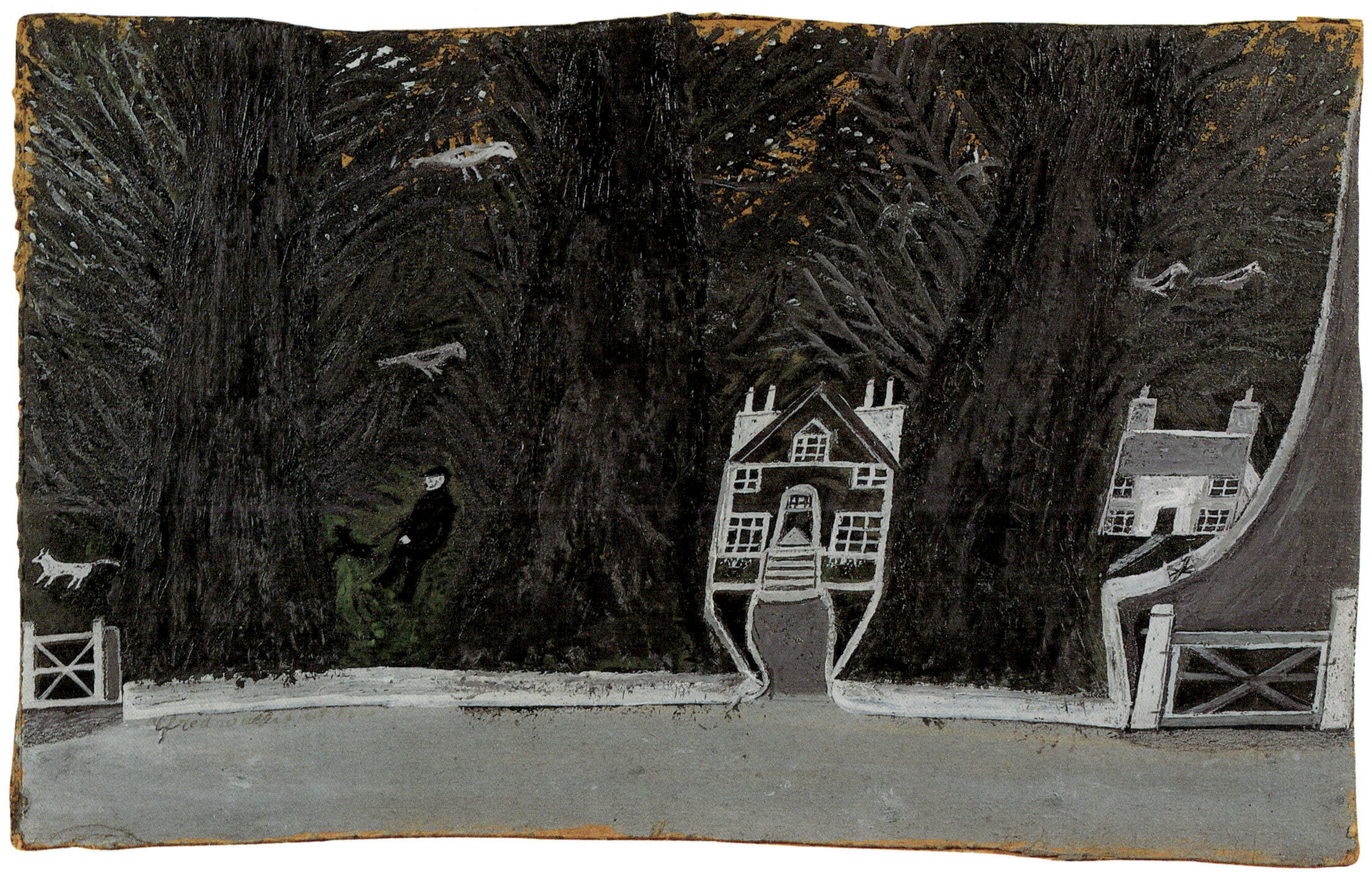

ABOVE Cottages in a wood, St. Ives

*RIGHT St. Ives. One of the few paintings that can be dated with any confidence —
c. 1928. It was given to Ben Nicholson by the artist when the two met for the first
time in that year. The irregular-shaped house in Porthmeor Square, visible from
Wallis' cottage in Back Road West, appears in a great many of his paintings*

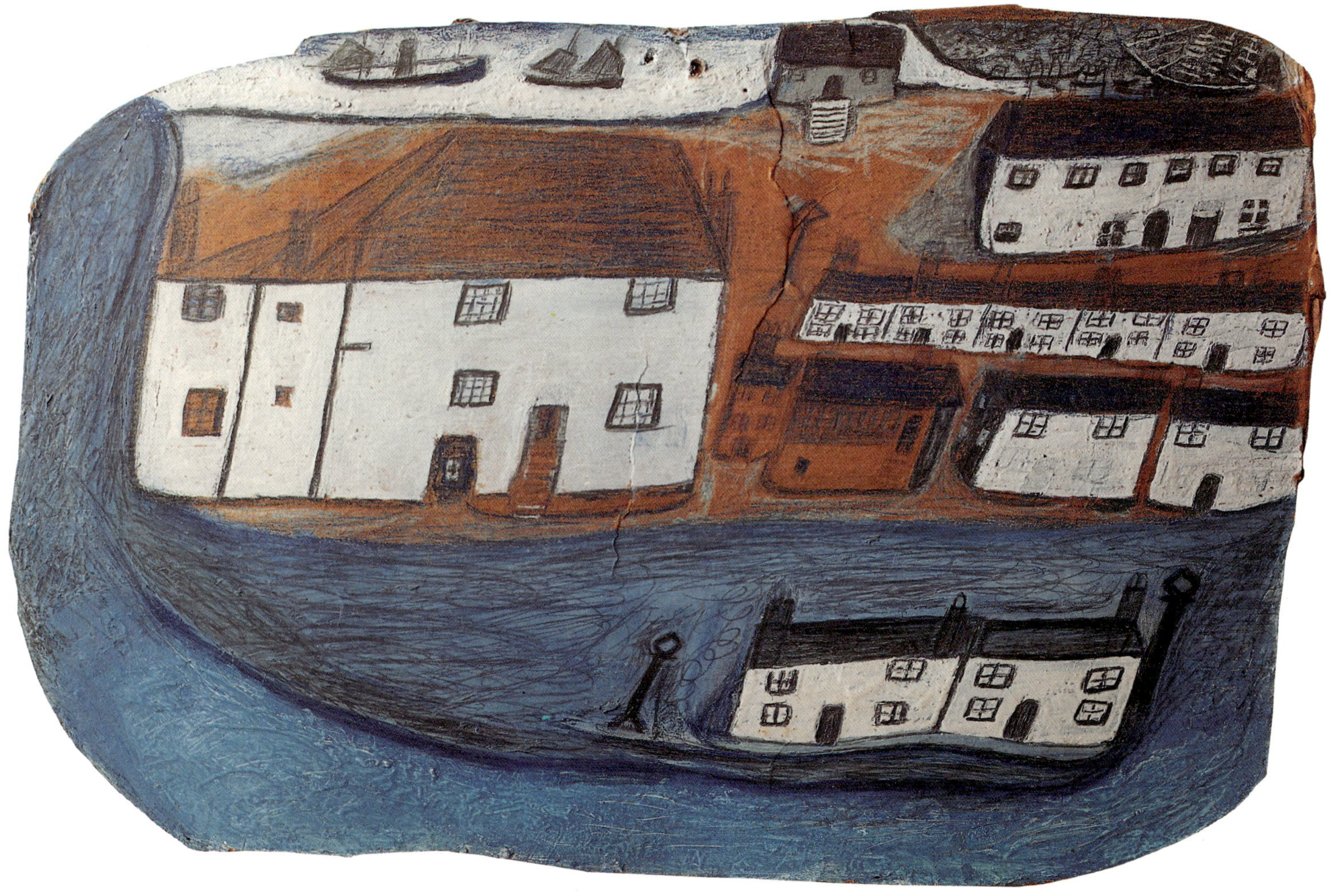

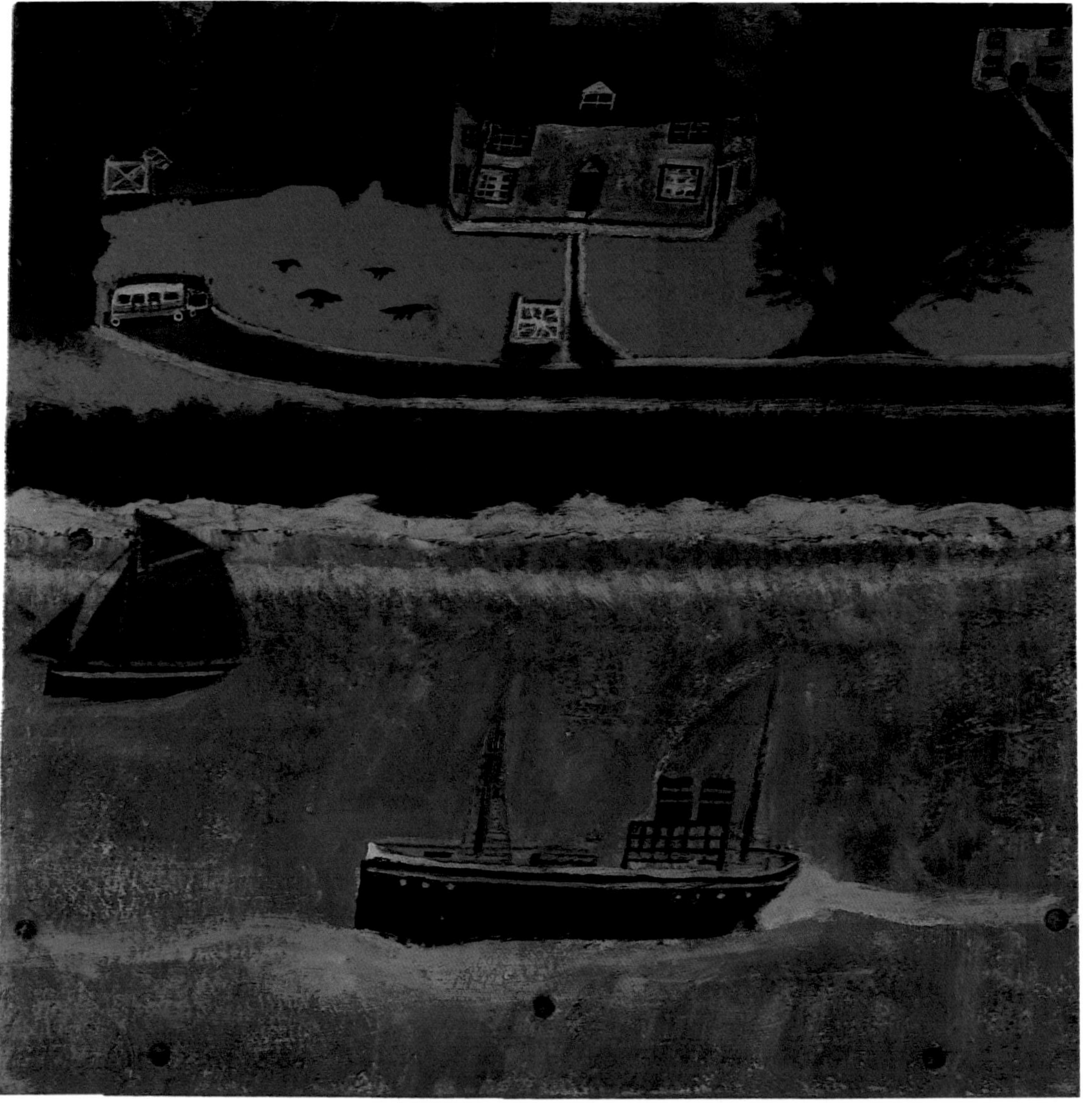

LEFT House and steamer

RIGHT Two-master and green
fields

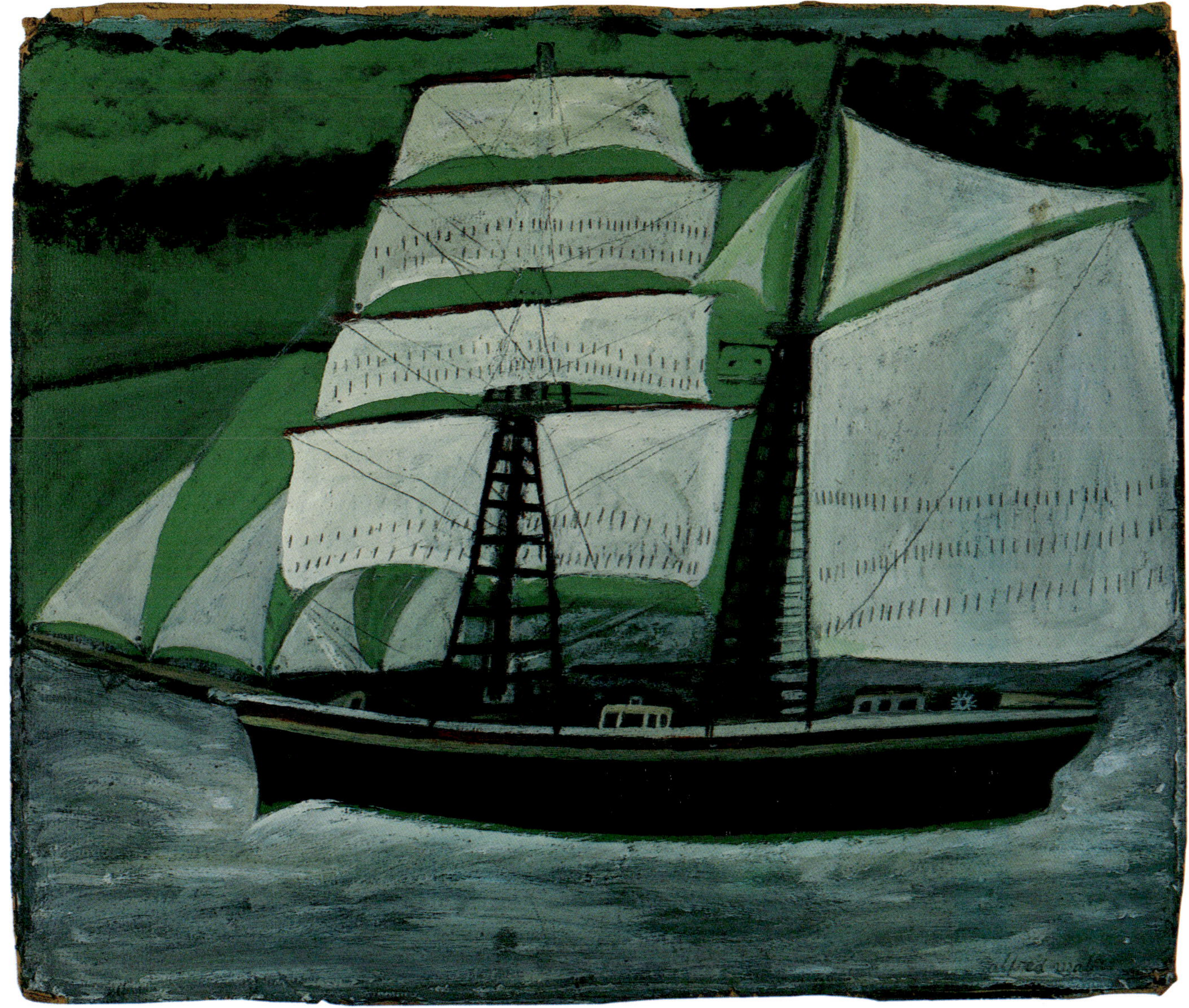

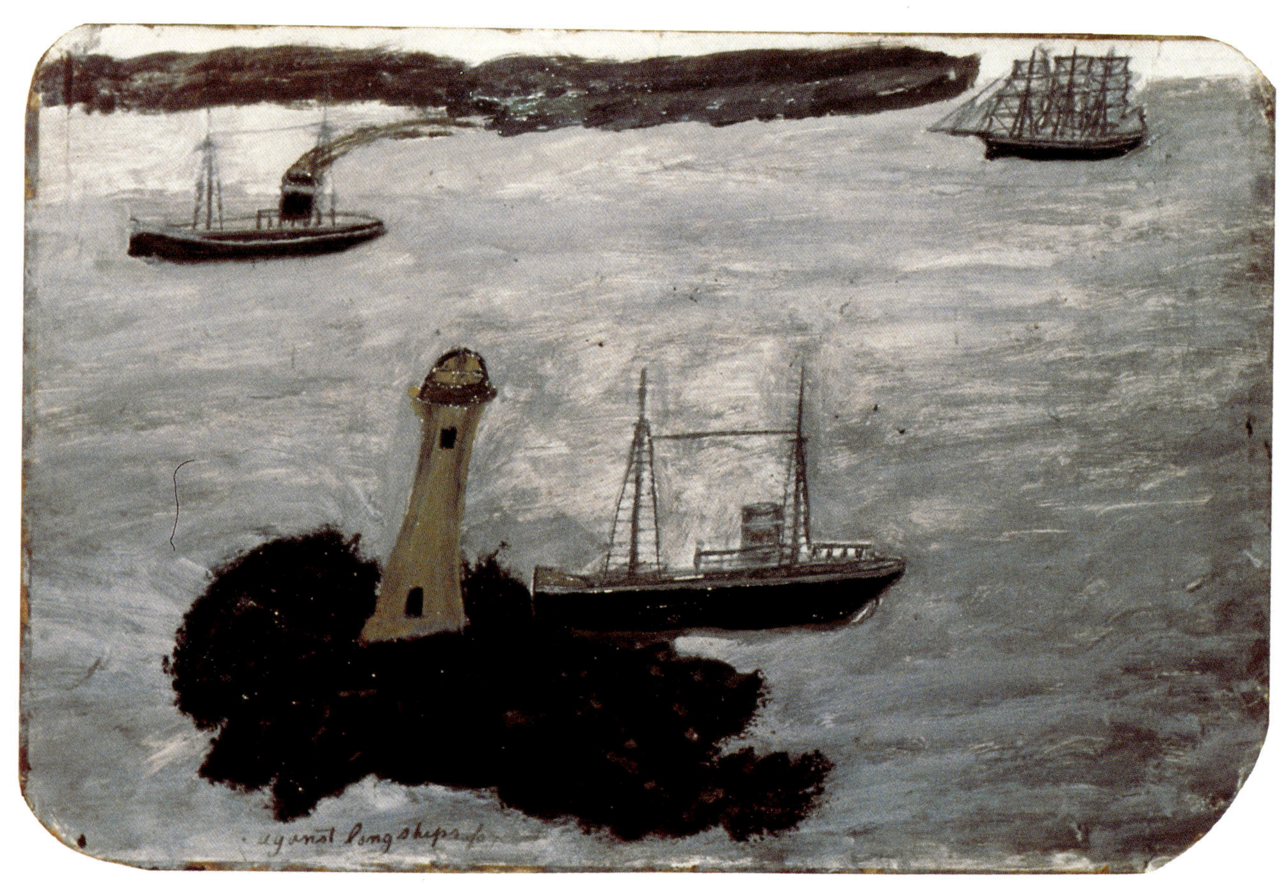

Three ships and lighthouse

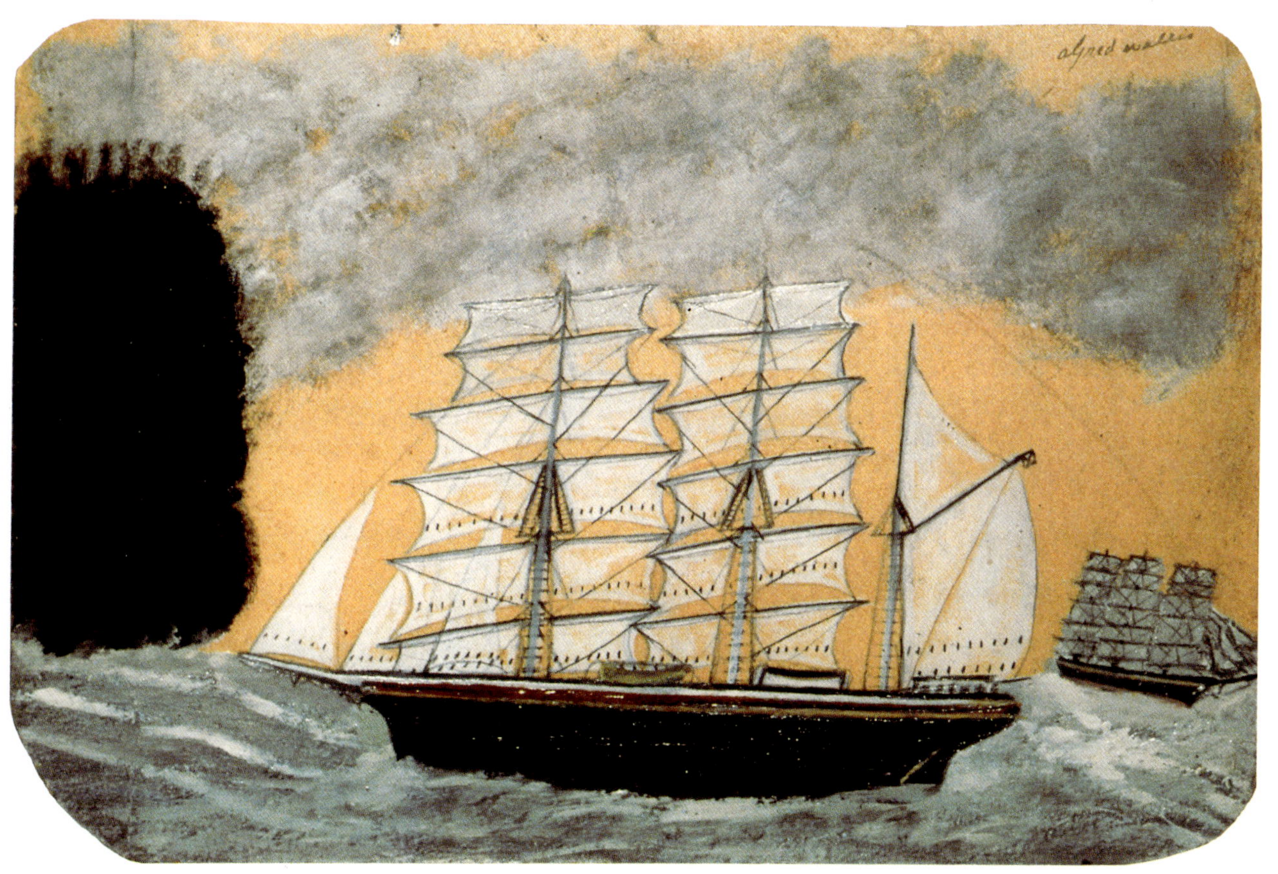

Headland with two three-masters

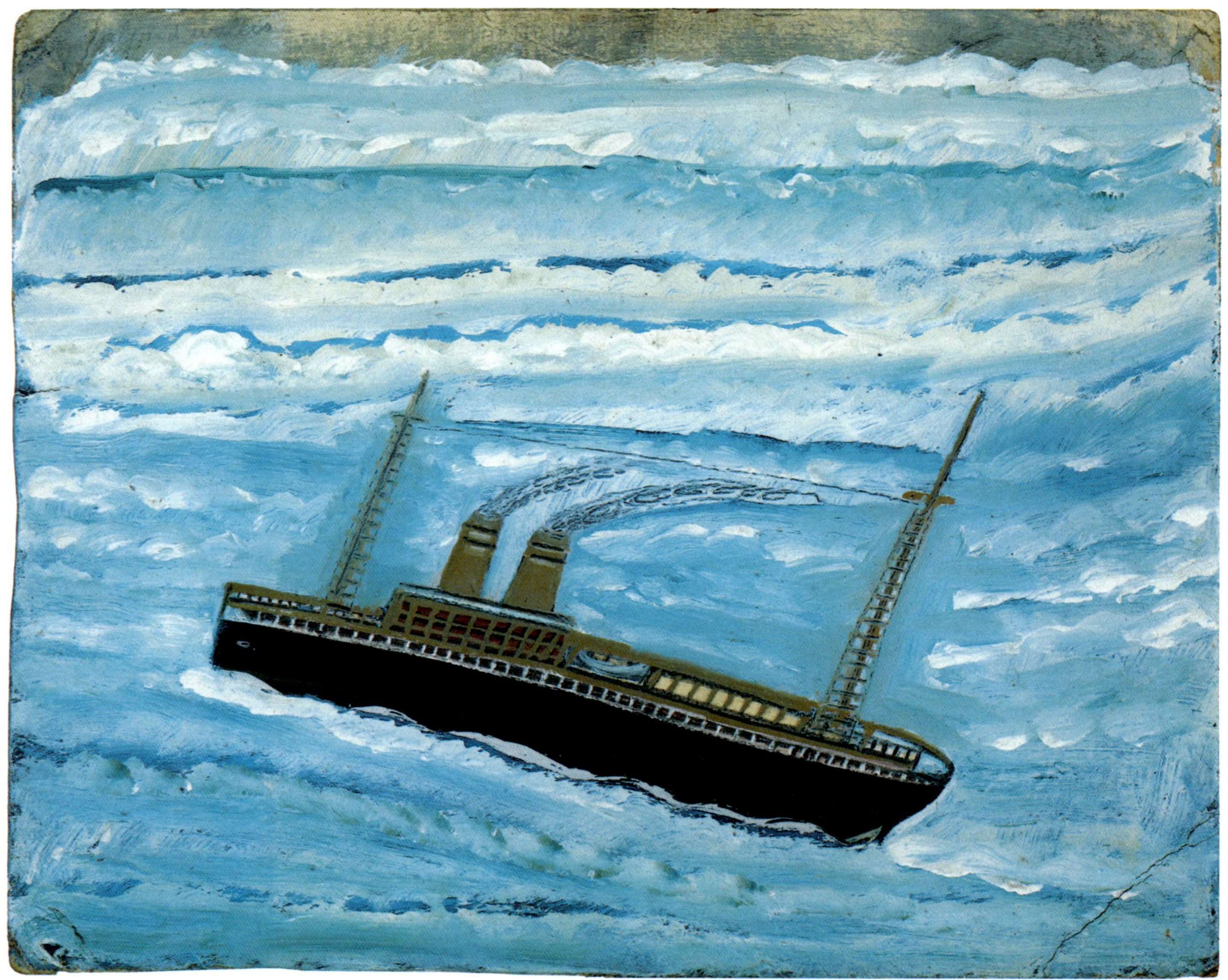

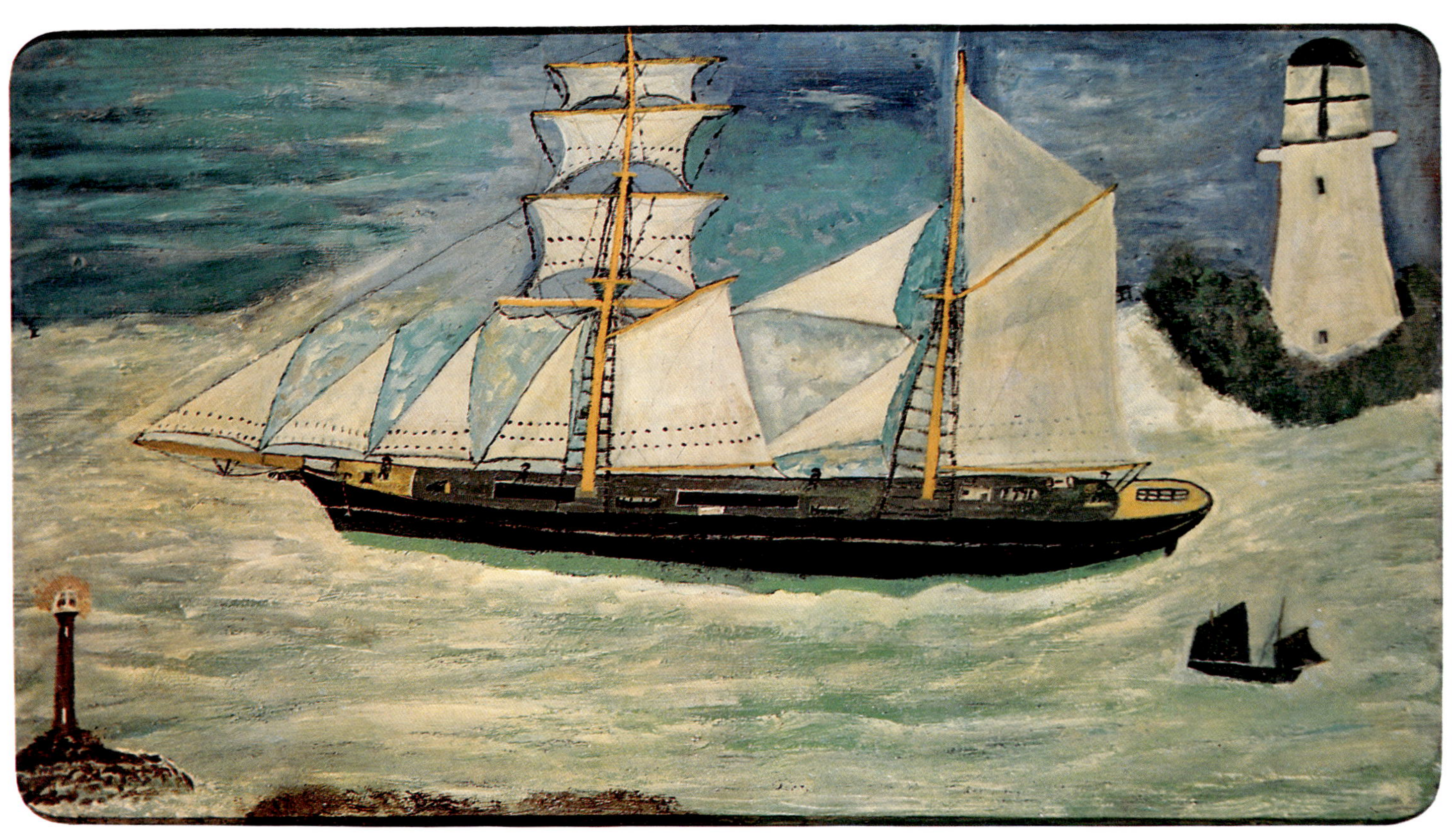

ABOVE Two-master with lighthouse. Painted on a wooden table-top, this is the largest of Wallis' surviving pictures, measuring 42" in length

Acknowledgements

pp.7–8. ex-collection; p.13. private collection, photograph by Bob Berry; p.14. private collection; p.17. ex-collection; p.18. private collection; p.20. private collection; p.22. Kettle's Yard, University of Cambridge; p.23. private collection; p.24. ex-collection; pp.26–8. Kettle's Yard, University of Cambridge; p.29. Arts Council Collection; p.30. Kettle's Yard, University of Cambridge; p.31. private collection; p.32. Kettle's Yard, University of Cambridge; p.33. Tate Gallery, London; p.34. ex-collection; p.35. private collection, photograph by Bob Berry; p.36. Mercury Gallery, London; p.37. ex-collection; p.38. private collection; p.39. Tate Gallery, London; p.40. private collection; p.41. ex-collection; p.42. Kettle's Yard, University of Cambridge; p.43. Pier Arts Centre, Stromness, Orkney; pp.44–5. Kettle's Yard, University of Cambridge; p.46. private collection; p.47. Mercury Gallery, London; pp.48–51. Kettle's Yard, University of Cambridge; pp.52–3. Pier Arts Centre, Stromness, Orkney; p.54. Kettle's Yard, University of Cambridge; p.55. ex-collection; p.56. Kettle's Yard, University of Cambridge; p.57. Tate Gallery, London; pp.58–9. Kettle's Yard, University of Cambridge; pp.60–1. Pier Arts Centre, Stromness, Orkney; p.62. Kettle's Yard, University of Cambridge; p.63. private collection.